SPIDER'S

A Play in Three Acts

by

AGATHA CHRISTIE

SAMUEL FRENCH

LONDON

NEW YORK SYDNEY TORONTO HOLLYWOOD

SPIDER'S WEB

Presented by Peter Saunders at the Savoy Theatre, London, on the 14th
December 1954, with the following cast of characters:

(in the order of their appearance)

SIR ROWLAND DELAHAYE	*Felix Aylmer*
HUGO BIRCH	*Harold Scott*
JEREMY WARRENDER	*Myles Eason*
CLARISSA HAILSHAM-BROWN	*Margaret Lockwood*
PIPPA HAILSHAM-BROWN, Clarissa's young step-daughter	*Margaret Barton*
MILDRED PEAKE	*Judith Furse*
ELGIN, the butler	*Sidney Monckton*
OLIVER COSTELLO	*Charles Morgan*
HENRY HAILSHAM-BROWN, Clarissa's husband	*John Warwick*
INSPECTOR LORD	*Campbell Singer*
CONSTABLE JONES	*Desmond Llewelyn*

The play directed by WALLACE DOUGLAS
Setting by MICHAEL WEIGHT

SYNOPSIS OF SCENES

*The action of the play passes in the drawing-room of Copplestone Court, the
Hailsham-Browns' home in Kent*

ACT I

An evening in March

ACT II

SCENE 1   A quarter of an hour later
SCENE 2   Ten minutes later

ACT III

A few minutes later

Time—the present

SPIDER'S WEB

ACT I

SCENE—*The drawing-room of Copplestone Court, the Hailsham-Browns' home in Kent. An evening in March.*

It is a charming and comfortable room with french windows down R *opening on to the garden. Double doors up* L *lead to the entrance hall where the foot of the staircase can be seen. A door up* LC *gives access to the library. In the left wall of the library a door leads to the entrance hall and in the right wall a window overlooks the garden. In the drawing-room a window up* R *also overlooks the garden. Up* RC *there is a concealed door or panel fitted with shelves. This is actuated by a small lever or switch in the right wall of a set of built-in bookshelves up* C. *The panel opens into the room and when open reveals a recess with a door in its back wall leading into the library. The room is furnished with good period furniture. There is a console table down* L *with a telephone on it, a console table up* C *beneath the bookshelves and a handsome period desk stands in the window up* R. *The upstage end of the desk is fitted with a secret drawer. There is a sofa* RC *with small tables* R *and* L *of it and a long stool below it. An armchair stands* LC *with an easy chair down* L *of it. A small table is between the two chairs. A desk stool and four upright chairs complete the furniture. At night the room is lit by concealed lighting behind the ceiling cornice and wall-brackets down* R, *up* RC, *up* LC *and down* L. *The concealed lighting is controlled by a switch above the hall doors and the brackets by a switch below the doors.*

(See the Ground Plan and Photograph of the Scene)

When the CURTAIN *rises, the console table* L *is at right angles to the wall* L *and on it there is a tray with three glasses of port marked one, two and three. Also on the table is a pencil and paper.* SIR ROWLAND DELAHAYE *is sitting on the left arm of the armchair. He is aged fifty odd, distinguished and with very definite charm. He is blindfolded and is sipping glass number two.* HUGO BIRCH *is standing* L *of Sir Rowland. He is aged about sixty and is a rather irascible type. He holds glass number three.* HUGO *and* SIR ROWLAND *are arguing.*

SIR ROWLAND (*tasting*) I should say—yes—definitely—yes, this is the Dow 'forty-two.

HUGO (*taking the glass from Sir Rowland*) Dow 'forty-two. (*He hands him the next glass then puts the first glass on the table and notes Sir Rowland's opinion*)

(SIR ROWLAND *sips the wine, sips again and nods affirmatively*)

SIR ROWLAND. Ah yes, this is a wine indeed. (*He sips*) Cockburn 'twenty-seven. To waste—(*he hands the glass to Hugo*) a bottle of Cockburn 'twenty-seven——

(HUGO *puts the glass on the table and writes*)

—on an experiment like this is positively sacrilegious. (*He rises, removes the blindfold and puts it on the back of his chair. He stands R of Hugo*)

HUGO (*reading his notes*) That, you say, is Cockburn 'twenty-seven. Number two was the Dow 'forty-two. Number one was— (*with disgust*) Rich Ruby port type wine. Pah! Can't think why Clarissa has such a thing in the house. My turn. (*He crosses below Sir Rowland, picks up the blindfold, hands it to Sir Rowland, and removes his spectacles*)

SIR ROWLAND (*moving behind Hugo and tying on the blindfold*) Probably uses it for jugged hare or for flavouring soup. There you are, Hugo. Ought to turn you round three times like they do in Blindman's Buff. (*He leads Hugo to R of the chair and turns him round*)

HUGO. Here, steady on.

SIR ROWLAND. Got it?

HUGO (*feeling for the chair*) Yes.

(SIR ROWLAND *seats* HUGO *in the chair then crosses to the table*)

SIR ROWLAND. I'll swivel the glasses round instead. (*He moves the glasses slightly*)

HUGO. No need to, think I'd be influenced by what you said? I'm as good a judge of port as you any day, Roly, my boy.

(JEREMY WARRENDER *enters by the french windows. He is an elegant young man and is wearing a raincoat. He is panting and out of breath and crosses quickly above the sofa to L of it*)

SIR ROWLAND. Can't be too careful. (*He picks up glass number three*)

JEREMY (*panting*) What's going on here? The three-card trick with glasses? (*He removes his raincoat and jacket*)

HUGO. Who's that? Who's brought a dog into the room?

SIR ROWLAND (*moving to L of Hugo, shouting*) It's only young Warrender.

HUGO. Oh, sounds like a dog that's been chasing a rabbit.

JEREMY. Three times to the lodge gates and back in a mackintosh. The Herzoslovakian Minister did it in four minutes fifty-three seconds. I went all out but couldn't do better than six minutes ten seconds. (*He falls on to the sofa*) I don't believe he did, either. Only Chris Chataway himself could do it in that time with or without a mackintosh.

SIR ROWLAND. Who told you that about the Herzoslovakian Minister?

JEREMY. Clarissa.

SIR ROWLAND. Clarissa!

HUGO (*snorting*) Oh, Clarissa. Don't you pay any attention to what Clarissa tells you.

SIR ROWLAND. I'm afraid you don't know your hostess very well, Warrender. She's a young lady with a very vivid imagination.

JEREMY (*rising*) Do you mean she made the whole thing up?

SIR ROWLAND (*handing glass number three to Hugo*) Well, I wouldn't put it past her.

JEREMY. You wait till I see that young woman. I'll have something to say to her. Gosh, I'm dead.

(JEREMY *crosses, exits to the hall, puts his raincoat on the stairs, and re-enters*)

HUGO. Stop puffing like a grampus. I want to concentrate. There's a fiver at stake. Roly and I have got a bet on.

(SIR ROWLAND *picks up glass number one*)

JEREMY (*crossing to* C) Oh, what is it?

HUGO. Who's the best judge of port. We've got Cockburn 'twenty-seven, Dow 'forty-two and the local grocer's special. Quiet now. This is important. (*He sips. Non-committal*) Mmm —ah.

(JEREMY *sits on the left arm of the sofa*)

SIR ROWLAND. Well?

HUGO. Don't hustle me, Roly—I'm not going to rush my fences. Where's the next one? (*He holds glass number three in his right hand*)

(SIR ROWLAND *hands glass number one to Hugo*)

(*He sips glass number one*) Yes, I'm pretty sure about those two. (*He hands glass number three to Sir Rowland*) This first one's the Dow. The second was the Cockburn. (*He hands glass number one to Sir Rowland*)

(SIR ROWLAND *puts the glass on the table and writes*)

SIR ROWLAND (*writing*) Number three the Dow. Number one the Cockburn.

HUGO. Hardly necessary to taste the third, but I suppose I'd better go through with it.

SIR ROWLAND (*handing Hugo glass number two*) Here you are.

HUGO (*sipping*) Tschah! Ugh! What unspeakable muck. (*He returns the glass to Sir Rowland and wipes his lips*)

(SIR ROWLAND *moves to the table*)

Take me an hour to get the taste out of my mouth. Here, get me out of this, Roly.

(SIR ROWLAND *sips the wine*)

JEREMY (*rising and moving behind Hugo*) I'll do it. (*He removes the blindfold*)

SIR ROWLAND. So that's what you say, is it? Number two grocer's special. Rubbish! It's the Dow 'forty-two, not a doubt of it.

(JEREMY *crosses above Sir Rowland to* L *of him*)

HUGO (*putting the blindfold in his pocket*) Pah! You've lost your palate, Roly.

JEREMY. Let me try. (*He takes a quick sip from each glass*) They all taste the same to me.

HUGO. You young people—it's all this confounded gin you're always drinking. Ruins your palate.

(CLARISSA HAILSHAM-BROWN *enters from the library*)

CLARISSA. Hello, my darlings. Have you settled it yet?

SIR ROWLAND. Yes, Clarissa. We're ready for you.

(CLARISSA *moves to* R *of Hugo*)

HUGO. Number one's the Cockburn, number two's the port type stuff, three's the Dow—right, eh?

SIR ROWLAND. Nonsense, number one's the port type stuff, two's the Dow, three's the Cockburn. I'm right, aren't I?

CLARISSA. Darlings. (*She kisses Hugo, then Sir Rowland*) Now, you take the tray back to the dining-room. (*She moves to the table up* C) You'll find the decanter on the sideboard. (*She takes a chocolate from the box on the table, then moves to the sofa*)

SIR ROWLAND (*picking up the tray with the glasses*) *The* decanter?

CLARISSA (*sitting on the sofa at the left end*) Yes, just one decanter. (*She puts her feet up*) It's all the same port, you know.

(JEREMY *laughs and crosses to* L *of the sofa.* HUGO *rises and stands behind the chair*)

SIR ROWLAND. Clarissa, you unprincipled humbug.

CLARISSA. Well, it's been such a wet afternoon and you meant to play golf. You must have some fun, and you have had fun over this, darlings, haven't you?

SIR ROWLAND. Upon my soul. You ought to be ashamed of yourself, showing up your elders and betters. (*He moves to ·the hall door*)

HUGO (*moving to the hall door; laughing*) Who was it said that he'd know Cockburn 'twenty-seven anywhere?

SIR ROWLAND. Never mind, Hugo, let's have some more.

(SIR ROWLAND *and* HUGO, *talking as they go, exit to the hall.* HUGO *closes the doors*)

JEREMY (*moving down* C) Now then, Clarissa, what's all this about the Herzoslovakian Minister?

CLARISSA. What about him?

JEREMY. Did he ever run to the lodge gates and back, in a mackintosh, three times in four minutes fifty-three seconds?

CLARISSA. The Herzoslovakian Minister is a dear, but he's well over sixty and I doubt very much if he's run anywhere for years.

JEREMY. So, you did make the whole thing up. Why?

CLARISSA. You've been complaining all day about not getting enough exercise.

JEREMY. Clarissa, do you ever speak the truth?

CLARISSA. Of course I do—sometimes. But when I am speaking the truth nobody ever seems to believe me. It's very odd. I suppose when you're making things up, you get carried away and that makes it sound more convincing. (*She rises and moves to the french windows*)

JEREMY. I might have broken a blood vessel. Fat lot you'd have cared about that.

CLARISSA (*laughing*) I do believe it's clearing up. It's going to be a lovely evening. How delicious the garden smells after rain. (*She sniffs*) Narcissus.

JEREMY. Do you really like living down here in the country?

CLARISSA. Love it.

JEREMY (*crossing above the sofa to Clarissa*) You must get bored to death. It's all so incongruous for you, Clarissa. You ought to lead a gay life in London.

CLARISSA (*crossing between the sofa and stool to* C) What—parties and night clubs?

JEREMY. You'd make a brilliant hostess.

CLARISSA (*moving above the armchair and turning to Jeremy*) It sounds like an Edwardian novel. Anyway, Diplomatic parties are terribly dull.

JEREMY (*crossing to Clarissa*) But it's such a waste. (*He tries to put his hand on hers*)

CLARISSA (*withdrawing her hand*) Of me?

JEREMY. Yes. Then there's Henry.

CLARISSA. What about Henry? (*She moves behind the easy chair and pats the cushion*)

JEREMY. I can't imagine why you ever married him. Years older than you, with a daughter at school. (*He leans on the armchair*) An excellent man, I have no doubt, but of all the pompous stuffed shirts. Going about looking like a boiled owl. (*He pauses*) Dull as ditchwater.

(*There is a pause, during which* CLARISSA *crosses below Jeremy to* C)

No sense of humour.

(CLARISSA *looks at Jeremy and smiles*)

Oh, I suppose you think I oughtn't to say these things.

A*

CLARISSA (*sitting on the right end of the stool*) Oh, I don't mind. Say anything you like.

JEREMY (*sitting L of Clarissa on the stool; eagerly*) So you do realize that you've made a mistake.

CLARISSA (*softly*) But I haven't made a mistake. (*Teasingly*) Are you making immoral advances to me, Jeremy?

JEREMY. Definitely.

CLARISSA. How lovely. Go on. (*She nudges him with her left elbow*)

JEREMY (*rising and turning to her*) I love you.

CLARISSA (*cheerfully*) I'm so glad.

JEREMY. That's entirely the wrong answer. You ought to say "I'm so sorry", in a deep, sympathetic voice.

CLARISSA. But I'm not sorry. I'm delighted. I *like* people to be in love with me.

(JEREMY *sits beside Clarissa, turned away in disgust*)

Would you do anything in the world for me?

JEREMY (*turning eagerly to her*) Anything.

CLARISSA. Really? Supposing I murdered someone, would you help . . . No, I must stop. (*She rises and moves behind the right end of the sofa*)

JEREMY (*turning on the stool to face her*) No, go on.

CLARISSA (*leaning over the right end of the sofa*) You said just now did I ever get bored.

JEREMY. Yes.

CLARISSA. Well, I suppose in a way I do, or rather I might if it wasn't for my private hobby.

JEREMY. Oh, what is it?

CLARISSA. You see, Jeremy, my life has always been peaceful and happy. Nothing exciting ever happened, so I began to play my little game. I call it "Supposing".

JEREMY. "Supposing"?

CLARISSA. Yes. (*She crosses behind the sofa to* C) I say to myself— supposing I were to come down one morning and find a dead body in the library, what should I do? Or supposing a woman were to be shown in here one day and told me that she and Henry had been secretly married in Constantinople, and that our marriage was bigamous, what should I say to her? Or sup- posing I had to choose between betraying my country and seeing Henry shot before my eyes? (*She smiles suddenly at Jeremy*) Or, even—(*she sits in the armchair*) supposing I were to run away with Jeremy, what would happen next?

JEREMY (*rising, crossing to Clarissa and kneeling beside her*) I feel flattered. What did happen? (*He takes her right hand*)

CLARISSA (*withdrawing her hand*) Well, the *last* time I played, we were on the Riviera at Juan les Pins, and Henry came after us. He had a revolver with him.

JEREMY. My God, did he shoot me?

CLARISSA. He said—(*dramatically*) "Clarissa, either you come back with me, or I kill myself".

JEREMY (*rising and moving down* C) Jolly decent of him. I can't imagine anything more unlike Henry. And what did you say to that?

CLARISSA (*smiling*) Well, I've played it both ways.

JEREMY (*moving above the armchair*) Well, darling, you certainly do have fun.

(PIPPA HAILSHAM-BROWN *enters from the hall. She is a lanky child aged twelve, wearing school clothes. She carries a satchel*)

PIPPA. Hullo, Clarissa.

(JEREMY *moves behind the sofa and sits on the back of it*)

CLARISSA. Hullo, Pippa. You're late.

PIPPA (*moving to the easy chair*) Music lesson. (*She puts her hat and satchel in the chair*) Any food about? I'm starving.

CLARISSA (*rising and moving behind the armchair*) Didn't you get your buns to eat in the bus?

PIPPA (*moving to* L *of Clarissa*) Oh, yes, but that was half an hour ago. Can't I have some cake or something to last me till supper?

CLARISSA (*leading Pippa to the hall door; laughing*) We'll see what we can find.

(CLARISSA *and* PIPPA *exit to the hall*)

PIPPA (*as they go*) Is there any of that cake with the cherries on top?

CLARISSA (*off*) No, you finished that yesterday.

(JEREMY *rises, moves to the desk and quickly opens and closes one or two of the drawers*)

MISS PEAKE (*off, loudly*) Ahoy there!

(JEREMY *starts and hastily closes the drawers. The daylight commences to fade as evening falls.*

MILDRED PEAKE *enters by the french windows. She is a big, jolly-looking woman of forty odd, in tweeds and gumboots*)

(*She stands on the window step*) Mrs Hailsham-Brown about?

JEREMY (*moving to* R *of the sofa*) Yes, she just went with Pippa to get her something to eat.

MISS PEAKE. Children shouldn't eat between meals.

JEREMY. Will you come in, Miss Peake?

MISS PEAKE. No, I won't come in because of my boots. (*She laughs*) Bring half the garden with me if I did. (*She laughs*) I just wanted to ask what veggies for tomorrow's lunch.

JEREMY. I'm afraid I . . .

MISS PEAKE. Tell you what, I'll come back. (*She turns to go, then turns back to Jeremy*) Oh, you will be careful of that desk, won't you, Mr. Warrender?

JEREMY. Yes, of course I will.

MISS PEAKE. It's a valuable antique. You oughtn't to wrench the drawers out like that.

JEREMY. I'm terribly sorry, I was only looking for notepaper.

MISS PEAKE. Middle pigeon-hole.

(JEREMY *turns to the desk, opens the middle pigeon-hole and extracts a sheet of writing-paper*)

That's right. Curious how often people can't see what's right in front of their eyes.

(MISS PEAKE *laughs heartily and exits by the french windows. JEREMY joins in her laughter, but stops abruptly when she has gone. PIPPA enters from the hall, munching a bun*)

PIPPA. Smashing bun. (*She closes the hall doors*)

JEREMY. Hullo, there. How was school today?

PIPPA (*moving to the table* LC) Pretty foul. (*She puts her bun on the table*) World affairs. (*She leans over the arm of the easy chair and opens her satchel*) Miss Wilkinson loves world affairs. She's terribly wet, can't keep order. (*She takes a book from her satchel*)

JEREMY. What's your favourite subject?

PIPPA. Biology. It's heaven.

(JEREMY *sits on the sofa at the left end*)

Yesterday we dissected a frog's leg. (*She crosses to Jeremy and pushes the book at his face*) Look what I got in the second-hand bookstall. (*She moves to the armchair and sits*) It's awfully rare, I'm sure. Over a hundred years old.

JEREMY. What is it, exactly?

PIPPA. It's a kind of recipe book. (*She opens the book*) It's thrilling, absolutely thrilling.

JEREMY. What's it all about?

PIPPA (*enthralled in her book*) What?

JEREMY (*rising*) It seems very absorbing.

PIPPA. What? (*To herself*) Gosh!

JEREMY (*moving below the stool*) Evidently a good tuppenny-worth. (*He picks up the newspaper from the stool*)

PIPPA. What's the difference between a wax candle and a tallow candle?

JEREMY. I should imagine that a tallow candle is markedly inferior. But surely you can't eat it?

PIPPA (*rising; much amused*) "Can you eat it?" Sounds like *Twenty Questions*. (*She laughs, throws the book on to the easy chair, moves up* C *and gets a pack of cards from the bottom shelf of the bookshelves up* C) Do you know demon patience? (*She moves down* C)

JEREMY (*engrossed in his paper*) Um.

PIPPA. I suppose you wouldn't like to play beggar-my-neighbour?

JEREMY. No. (*He replaces the paper on the stool, then moves to the desk, sits and addresses an envelope*)

PIPPA. I thought you wouldn't. I wish we could have a fine day for a change. (*She kneels on the floor down C, lays out her cards and plays demon patience*) Such a waste being in the country, when it's wet.

JEREMY. Do you like living in the country?

PIPPA. Rather. I like it much better than living in London. This is a wizard house with a tennis court and everything. We've even got a priest's hole.

JEREMY. A priest's hole, in this house?

PIPPA. Yes.

JEREMY. Don't believe it. Wrong period.

PIPPA. Well, *I* call it a priest's hole. Look, I'll show you. (*She rises, moves to the right end of the bookshelves up C, takes out a book and pulls down a small lever in the right wall of the shelves*)

(*The concealed door between the bookshelves and the window up RC swings open, revealing a good sized recess, with a concealed door in its back wall, leading to the library*)

It isn't really a priest's hole, of course. Actually that door goes through into the library.

JEREMY (*rising and moving to the recess*) Oh, does it? (*He goes into the recess, opens the door in the back, glances into the library and closes the door*) So it does. (*He comes into the room*)

PIPPA. But it's all rather secret and you'd never guess it was there unless you knew. (*She lifts the lever*)

(*The panel closes*)

I'm using it all the time. It's the sort of place that would be very convenient for putting a dead body, don't you think?

JEREMY. Absolutely made for it.

(PIPPA *moves down C, kneels and resumes her game.*
CLARISSA *enters from the hall and moves to the table LC*)

(*To Clarissa*) The Amazon is looking for you.

CLARISSA. Miss Peake? Oh, what a bore. (*She picks up Pippa's bun, takes a bite and moves above Pippa to L of the sofa*)

PIPPA (*rising*) Hey! That's mine!

CLARISSA. Greedy thing. (*She hands the bun to Pippa*)

(PIPPA *puts the bun on the table LC, then kneels and resumes her game*)

JEREMY. First she hailed me as though I were a ship, then ticked me off for manhandling this desk.

CLARISSA (*leaning over the left end of the sofa*) She's a terrible pest, but she goes with the house—(*to Pippa*) black ten on the red jack—(*to Jeremy*) and she's really a very good gardener.

JEREMY. I know. (*He moves to* R *of Clarissa and puts his arm around her*) I saw her out of my bedroom window this morning digging something that looked like an enormous grave.

CLARISSA. That's deep trenching.

JEREMY (*to Pippa*) Red three on the black four.

> (PIPPA *looks furious*.
> SIR ROWLAND *and* HUGO *enter from the library*. SIR ROWLAND *looks at* JEREMY, *who moves away from Clarissa to* R)

SIR ROWLAND. Seems to have cleared at last. Too late for golf, though. (*He moves to* L *of Pippa*) Only about twenty minutes' daylight left. (*He points with his foot at a card. To Pippa*) Look, that goes on there. (*He crosses to the french windows*) Well, I suppose we might as well go across to the golf house.

HUGO (*moving behind Pippa*) I'll go and get my coat. (*He leans over Pippa to point out a card*)

> (PIPPA, *furious, leans forward and covers the cards with her body*)

(*To Jeremy*) What about you, my boy?

JEREMY (*crossing to the hall door*) I'll have to get my jacket.

> (HUGO *and* JEREMY *exit to the hall, leaving the door open*. JEREMY *goes up the stairs, passing* ELGIN *coming down*)

CLARISSA (*to Sir Rowland*) Sure you don't mind dining at the club house, darling?

SIR ROWLAND (*moving to* R *of Clarissa*) Not a bit. Very sensible arrangement as the servants are going out.

> (ELGIN, *a middle-aged butler, enters from the hall*)

ELGIN (*moving up* L) Your supper is ready in the schoolroom, Miss Pippa.

PIPPA (*springing up*) Oh, good! I'm *ravenous*. (*She darts towards the hall door*)

CLARISSA. Here, here, you put those cards away first.

PIPPA. Oh, bother. (*She moves down* C, *kneels and slowly shovels the cards into a heap against the left end of the sofa. During the ensuing speeches, she slowly stacks up the cards, but leaves the Ace of Spades just under the left end of the sofa*)

ELGIN. Excuse me, madam.

CLARISSA (*crossing to* R *of Elgin*) Yes, Elgin, what is it?

ELGIN. There has been a little—er—unpleasantness, over the vegetables.

CLARISSA. Oh, dear. With Miss Peake?

ELGIN. Yes, madam. Mrs Elgin finds Miss Peake most difficult, madam. She is continually coming into the kitchen and criticizing and making remarks, and Mrs Elgin doesn't like it, she doesn't like it at all. Wherever we have been, Mrs Elgin and myself have always had very pleasant relations with the garden.

CLARISSA. I'm very sorry. I'll—er—I'll try to arrange it.

ELGIN. Thank you, madam.

(ELGIN *exits to the hall, closing the doors behind him*)

CLARISSA (*moving above the armchair*) How tiresome they are, and what curious things they say. How can one have pleasant relations with the garden? It sounds improper, in a pagan kind of way.

SIR ROWLAND. You're lucky with this couple you've got. Where did you get them?

CLARISSA. Registry Office.

SIR ROWLAND. I hope not that what's-its-name one where they always send you crooks.

PIPPA. Cooks?

SIR ROWLAND. No, crooks.

CLARISSA. Come on, Pippa, hurry up.

PIPPA (*picking up the cards, rising and moving up* c) There! (*She replaces the cards on the bookshelves*) I wish one didn't always have to do clearing up. (*She moves to the hall door*)

CLARISSA (*picking up the bun from the table* LC) Here, take your bun with you. (*She hands the bun to Pippa*)

(PIPPA *starts to go*)

And your satchel.

(PIPPA *runs to the easy chair, snatches up her satchel and turns towards the hall door*)

Hat!

(PIPPA *puts the bun on the table* LC, *picks up her hat and runs to the hall door*)

Here! (*She picks up the bun, moves to Pippa, stuffs the bun in her mouth, takes the hat, jams it on Pippa's head and pushes her into the hall*) And shut the door.

(PIPPA *exits to the hall, closing the doors behind her. The light in the room begins to fade a little.* SIR ROWLAND *laughs.* CLARISSA *joins in the laughter, crosses to the table* L *of the sofa and takes a cigarette from the box on it*)

SIR ROWLAND. Wonderful. She's a different child. You've done a good job there, Clarissa.

CLARISSA (*sitting on the sofa at the left end*) I think she really likes me now, and trusts me. I quite enjoy being a stepmother.

SIR ROWLAND (*lighting Clarissa's cigarette from the lighter on the table* L *of the sofa*) She seems a normal, happy child again.

CLARISSA. I think living in the country has made all the difference, and she goes to a very nice school and is making lots of friends there. Yes, I think she's happy, and as you say, *normal*.

SIR ROWLAND (*crossing below the stool to* R *of it*) It's a shocking thing to see a kid get into the state she was in. I'd like to wring Miranda's neck.

CLARISSA. Pippa was absolutely terrified of her mother.

SIR ROWLAND (*sitting* R *of Clarissa on the sofa*) A shocking business.

CLARISSA. I feel furious every time I think of Miranda. What she made Henry suffer and what she made that child go through. I still can't understand how any woman *could*.

SIR ROWLAND. Taking drugs is a nasty business. It alters your whole character.

CLARISSA. Well, what started her on them in the first place?

SIR ROWLAND. I think it was that swine Oliver Costello. I believe he's in on the drug racket.

CLARISSA. He's a horrible man. Really evil, I always think.

SIR ROWLAND. She's married him, hasn't she?

CLARISSA. About a month ago.

SIR ROWLAND. Well, Henry's well rid of Miranda. He's a nice fellow, Henry. (*Emphatically*) A really nice fellow.

CLARISSA (*gently*) Do you think you need to tell me that?

SIR ROWLAND. He doesn't say much. Undemonstrative—but he's sound all through. (*He pauses*) That young fellow, Jeremy what's-his-name. What do you know about him?

CLARISSA (*smiling*) He's very amusing.

SIR ROWLAND. Ptscha! That's all people seem to care about these days. Don't—don't do anything foolish, will you?

CLARISSA. Don't fall in love with Jeremy Warrender. That's what you mean?

SIR ROWLAND. That would be extremely foolish. You know, Clarissa darling, I've watched you grow up. You really mean a great deal to me. If ever you're in trouble of any kind, you would come to your old guardian, wouldn't you?

CLARISSA. Of course, Roly darling. (*She kisses him*) And you needn't worry about Jeremy.

(MISS PEAKE *enters by the french windows. She is in her stockinged feet and carries a head of broccoli*)

MISS PEAKE. I hope you don't mind my coming in this way, Mrs Brown-Hailsham. (*She moves above the sofa*) I shan't make the room dirty, I've left my boots outside. I'd just like you to look at this broccoli. (*She puts it over the back of the sofa in a belligerent manner and sticks it under Clarissa's nose*)

CLARISSA. It—er—it looks very nice.

MISS PEAKE (*thrusting the broccoli under Sir Rowland's nose*) Take a look.

Sir Rowland (*surveying the broccoli*) I can't see anything wrong with it. (*He takes the broccoli from her*)
Miss Peake. Of course there's nothing wrong with it. I took in just such another yesterday and that woman in the kitchen—of course, I don't want to say anything against your servants, Mrs Hailsham-Brown, though I *could* say a great deal—but that Mrs Elgin actually told me that it was such a poor specimen she wasn't going to cook it. She said something about "If you can't do better than *that* in the kitchen garden you'd better take up some other job". I was so angry I could have killed her.

(Clarissa *starts to speak*)

I never want to make trouble, but I'm *not* going into the kitchen to be insulted. In future I shall leave the vegetables outside the back door and Mrs Elgin can leave a list there——

(Sir Rowland *lifts up the broccoli*)

(*she ignores Sir Rowland*)—of what is required.

(*The telephone rings*)

(*She crosses above the armchair to the telephone*) I'll answer it. (*She lifts the receiver. Into the telephone*) Hullo . . . Yes . . . (*She wipes the top of the table with a corner of her overall*) Copplestone Court . . . You want Mrs Brown? . . . Yes—she's here. (*She holds out the receiver*)

(Clarissa *rises, stubs out her cigarette, crosses below the chairs, and takes the receiver*)

Clarissa (*into the telephone*) This is Mrs Hailsham—— Hullo . . . Hullo . . . How odd! They seem to have rung off. (*She replaces the receiver*)

(Miss Peake *suddenly moves forward and sets the console table* L *back against the wall*)

Miss Peake. Excuse me, but Mr Sellon always liked this table flat against the wall.

(Clarissa *assists* Miss Peake *with the table*)

Thank you, and you will be careful about marks made with—(*she moves behind the armchair*) glasses on the furniture——

(Clarissa *looks anxiously at the table*)

won't you, Mrs Brown-Hailsham—I mean Mrs Hailsham-Brown. (*She laughs in a hearty fashion*) Oh well, Brown-Hailsham, Hailsham-Brown, it's really all the same thing, isn't it? (*She moves* c)
Sir Rowland (*with distinct enunciation*) No, it's not. A horse chestnut is hardly the same thing as a chestnut horse.

(Miss Peake *laughs heartily*.
Hugo *enters from the hall*)

MISS PEAKE (*to Hugo*) I'm getting a regular ticking off. Quite sarcastic. (*She thumps Hugo on the back*) Well, good night, all. (*She moves behind the sofa*) I must be toddling back. Give me the broccoli.

(SIR ROWLAND *hands the broccoli to Miss Peake*)

Horse chestnut, chestnut horse. Jolly good—I must remember that.

(MISS PEAKE *laughs and exits by the french windows*)

HUGO (*crossing to* C) How does Henry bear that woman?

CLARISSA (*picking up Pippa's book from the easy chair and putting it on the table* LC) He finds her very hard to take. (*She sits in the easy chair*)

HUGO. I should think so. So damned arch! All that hearty schoolgirl manner.

SIR ROWLAND. A case of arrested development, I'm afraid.

CLARISSA. I agree she's maddening but she's a very good gardener, and she goes with the house, and since the house is so wonderfully cheap . . .

HUGO. Cheap? Is it? You surprise me.

CLARISSA. Marvellously cheap. It was advertised. We came down and saw it and took it then and there for six months furnished.

SIR ROWLAND. Who does it belong to?

CLARISSA. It belonged to a Mr Sellon. He died. He was an antique dealer in Maidstone.

HUGO. That's right. Sellon and Brown. I once bought a very nice Chippendale mirror there. Sellon lived here and used to go into Maidstone every day, but I believe he sometimes brought customers out here.

CLARISSA. Mind you, there are one or two disadvantages about the house. Only yesterday a man in a violent check suit drove up in a sports car and wanted to buy that desk. I told him it wasn't ours and we couldn't sell it, but he simply wouldn't believe me and kept on raising the price. He went up to five hundred pounds in the end.

SIR ROWLAND (*startled*) Five hundred pounds! (*He rises and moves to the upstage end of the desk*) Good Lord! Why, even at the Antique Dealers' Fair . . .

(HUGO *moves above the sofa.*
PIPPA *enters from the hall and moves above the armchair*)

PIPPA. I'm still hungry.

CLARISSA. You can't be.

PIPPA. I am. Milk and chocolate biscuits and a banana aren't really filling. (*She sits over the right arm of the armchair*)

Sir Rowland. It's a nice desk, quite genuine, but not what I'd call a collector's piece.

Hugo. Perhaps it's got a secret drawer with a diamond necklace in it.

Pippa. It has got a secret drawer.

Clarissa. What!

Pippa. I found a book in the market all about secret drawers in old furniture and I tried all over the house, but this is the only one that's got one. (*She rises*) Look, I'll show you. (*She crosses to the desk and operates it from the upstage drawer*)

(Clarissa *rises, crosses and kneels on the sofa, leaning over the back*)

(*She lifts the flap and takes out a drawer*) See, you slide out this and there's a sort of little catch thing underneath.

Hugo. Humph! Not very secret.

Pippa. Ah, but that's not all. Underneath there's a spring—and a drawer flies out. (*She demonstrates and a small drawer shoots out of the desk*) See!

(Hugo *takes the second drawer and picks a piece of paper out of it*)

Hugo. Hullo, what's inside? (*He reads*) "Sucks to you!"

(Pippa *goes off into a gale of laughter*)

Sir Rowland. What!

(*They all laugh and* Sir Rowland *shakes* Pippa, *who punches him*)

Pippa (*putting the drawers on the desk*) I put that there.

Sir Rowland. Villain!

Pippa. Actually, there was an envelope with an autograph of Queen Victoria in it. Look, I'll show you. (*She dashes to the bookshelves up* c)

(Clarissa *rises, moves to the desk, replaces the drawers and closes the flap.* Pippa *opens a shell box on the lower shelf of the bookcase, takes out an old envelope containing three scraps of paper and displays them*)

Sir Rowland. Do you collect autographs, Pippa?

Pippa. Not really. Only as a side line. (*She hands one autograph to Hugo*)

(Hugo *looks at the autograph and passes it to Sir Rowland*)

A girl at school collects stamps and her brother's got a smashing collection himself. Last Autumn he thought he'd got one like the one in the paper—— (*She hands another autograph to Hugo*)

(Hugo *passes the autograph to Sir Rowland*)

—a Swedish something or other which was worth hundreds of pounds. (*She hands the remaining autograph and the envelope to Hugo*)

(HUGO *passes the autograph and envelope to Sir Rowland*)

He was awfully excited and took it to a dealer, but the dealer said it wasn't what he thought it was, but it was quite a good stamp. Anyway, he gave him five pounds for it.

(SIR ROWLAND *hands two autographs to* HUGO *who passes them to Pippa*)

Five pounds is pretty good, isn't it?

(HUGO *grunts agreement*)

(*She looks down at the autographs*) How much is Queen Victoria's autograph worth?

SIR ROWLAND (*looking at the envelope*) About five to ten shillings, I should think.

PIPPA. There's Ruskin's here too, and Robert Browning's.

SIR ROWLAND (*returning the remaining autograph and envelope to Hugo*) Not much either, I'm afraid.

(HUGO *hands the autograph and envelope to Pippa*)

PIPPA. I wish I had Neville Duke's and Roger Bannister's. These historical ones are rather mouldy, I think. (*She replaces the envelope and autograph in the box, then backs to the hall door*) Can I see if there are any more chocolate biscuits in the larder, Clarissa?

CLARISSA. Yes. If you like.

HUGO. We must get off. (*He follows Pippa towards the door and calls*) Jeremy! Hi! Jeremy!

JEREMY (*off, calling*) Coming.

(JEREMY *enters down the stairs. He carries a golf club*)

CLARISSA. Henry ought to be back soon.

(JEREMY *comes into the room by the hall door*)

HUGO (*crossing to the french windows*) Better go out this way. It's nearer. Good night, Clarissa. Thank you for your hospitality.

JEREMY (*crossing to the french windows*) Good night, Clarissa.

(HUGO *and* JEREMY *exit by the french windows.* CLARISSA *acknowledges their "good nights"*)

SIR ROWLAND (*moving to Clarissa and putting his arm around her*) Good night. Warrender and I will probably not be in until about midnight.

(CLARISSA *and* SIR ROWLAND *move towards the french windows*)

CLARISSA. It's really a lovely evening. I'll come with you as far as the gate on to the golf course.

(CLARISSA *and* SIR ROWLAND *exit by the french windows.*
ELGIN *enters from the hall. He carries a tray of drinks which he
puts on the table up* C. *The front door bell rings off.*
ELGIN *exits to the hall, leaving the door open*)

ELGIN (*off*) Good evening, sir.
OLIVER (*off*) I've come to see Mrs Brown.
ELGIN (*off*) Oh yes, sir.

(*The front door is heard to close*)

What name, sir?
OLIVER (*off*) Mr Costello.
ELGIN (*off*) This way, sir.

(ELGIN *enters from the hall and stands to one side.*
OLIVER COSTELLO *enters from the hall and crosses to* C. *He is
a theatrically handsome, dark man with a rather unpleasant face*)

If you'll wait here, sir. Madam is at home. I'll see if I can find
her. (*He starts to go then stops and turns*) Mr Costello, did you say?
OLIVER. That's right. *Oliver* Costello.
ELGIN. Very good, sir.

(ELGIN *exits to the hall, closing the door.* OLIVER *looks around the
room, listens at the hall door, and the library door, then crosses to
the desk. He bends over it and looks at the drawers. He apparently hears
something and crosses to* C.
CLARISSA *enters by the french windows.* OLIVER *turns, surprised*)

CLARISSA (*standing on the window step; with intense surprise*) You?
OLIVER (*moving to* L *of the sofa, appearing equally surprised*)
Clarissa! What are you doing here?
CLARISSA. That's a rather silly question, isn't it? It's my house.
OLIVER. This is your house?
CLARISSA. Don't pretend you don't know.
OLIVER (*in an unpleasantly familiar manner*) It's charming—used
to belong to old what's-his-name, the antique dealer, didn't it?
He brought me out here once to show me some Louis Quinze
chairs. (*He takes his cigarette case from his pocket*) Cigarette?
CLARISSA. No, thank you. And I think you'd better go. My
husband will be home quite soon and I don't think he'll be very
pleased to see you.
OLIVER (*moving behind the armchair; with rather insolent amusement*)
But I particularly do want to see him. That's why I've come
here, really, to discuss suitable arrangements . . .
CLARISSA (*moving behind the sofa*) Arrangements?
OLIVER. For Pippa. Miranda's quite agreeable to Pippa's
spending part of the Summer holidays with Henry, and perhaps
a week at Christmas. But otherwise . . .

CLARISSA (*interrupting him sharply*) What do you mean? Pippa's home is here.

OLIVER (*moving to the table up* C) But, my dear Clarissa, you're surely aware that the court gave Miranda the custody of the child? (*He picks up a bottle of whisky*) May I? (*He pours a drink for himself*) The case was undefended, remember?

CLARISSA. Henry allowed Miranda to divorce him, but it was agreed between them privately that Pippa should live with her father. If Miranda had not agreed to that, Henry would have divorced *her*.

OLIVER (*moving to* L *of Clarissa*) You don't know Miranda well, do you? She so often changes her mind.

CLARISSA (*turning away with a step to* R) I don't believe for one moment that Miranda wants that child or cares twopence about her.

OLIVER (*with impertinence*) But you're not a mother, my dear Clarissa. You don't mind my calling you Clarissa, do you? After all, now I'm married to Miranda we're practically relations-in-law. (*He swallows his drink in one gulp then moves to the table up* C *and puts his glass on it*) Yes, I can assure you, Miranda is feeling violently maternal.

CLARISSA (*turning to him*) I don't believe it.

OLIVER (*moving to the armchair and sitting*) Please yourself. After all, there was no arrangement in writing, you know.

CLARISSA. You're not going to have Pippa. The child was a nervous wreck. She's better now, and happy at school, and that's the way she's going to remain.

OLIVER. How will you manage that, my dear? The law is on our side.

CLARISSA (*crossing to* R *of Oliver*) What's behind all this? What do you really want? Oh! What a fool I am. Of course, it's blackmail.

(ELGIN *enters abruptly from the hall*)

ELGIN. I was looking for you, madam.

(CLARISSA *moves below the right end of the sofa*)

Will it be quite all right for us to leave now, madam?

CLARISSA. Yes, quite all right, Elgin.

ELGIN. The taxi has come for us. Supper is laid all ready in the dining-room. (*He turns to go, then turns back to Clarissa*) Do you want me to shut up in here, madam? (*He eyes Oliver*)

CLARISSA. No, I'll see to it.

ELGIN. Thank you, madam. (*He goes to the hall door*) Good night, madam.

CLARISSA. Good night, Elgin.

(ELGIN *exits to the hall*)

OLIVER. Blackmail is a very ugly word, Clarissa. Have I mentioned money?

CLARISSA (*moving behind the sofa*) Not yet, but that's what you mean, isn't it?

OLIVER. It's true that we're not very well off. Miranda, you know, has always been extravagant. I think she feels that Henry might be able to spare her a somewhat larger allowance. After all, he's a rich man.

CLARISSA (*crossing to R of Oliver*) Now listen. I don't know about Henry, but I do know about myself. You try to get Pippa away from here and I'll fight you tooth and nail, and I don't care what weapons I use.

(OLIVER *chuckles*)

It shouldn't be difficult to get medical evidence proving Miranda's a drug addict. I'd even go to Scotland Yard and talk to the Narcotic Squad, and I'd suggest they kept an eye on *you*.

OLIVER (*sitting up*) Henry will hardly care for your methods.

CLARISSA. Then Henry will have to lump them. It's the child that matters. I'm not going to have Pippa bullied or frightened.

(PIPPA *enters from the hall*)

PIPPA (*as she enters*) Clarissa—(*she crosses above the armchair to* R *of Oliver*) did you know there were only two chocolate biscuits in the tin? (*She sees Oliver, stops short and looks terrified*)

OLIVER. Why, hullo, Pippa.

(PIPPA *backs towards the table* L)

How you've grown. (*He rises and moves towards Pippa*)

(PIPPA *backs down* L)

I've just come to make some arrangements about you. Your mother is looking forward to having you with her again. She and I are married now and . . .

PIPPA (*running to Clarissa, hysterically*) I won't come. I won't come. Clarissa.

CLARISSA (*putting her arm around Pippa*) Don't worry, Pippa. Your home is here with your father and with me and you're not leaving it.

OLIVER (*moving to* L *of Pippa*) But I assure you . . .

CLARISSA. Get out of here at once.

(OLIVER, *mockingly afraid of Clarissa, backs* R, *above the stool*)

At once. (*She moves towards him*) I won't have you in my house, do you hear?

(MISS PEAKE *enters by the french windows. She carries a large garden-fork*)

MISS PEAKE. Oh, Mrs Brown-Hailsham, I . . .

CLARISSA. Miss Peake. Will you show Mr Costello the way through the garden to the gate on to the links?

(OLIVER *looks at Miss Peake.* MISS PEAKE *lifts the fork in her downstage arm*)

OLIVER. Miss—Peake?

MISS PEAKE (*robustly*) Pleased to meet you. I'm the gardener here.

OLIVER. Indeed. I came here once before to look at some antique furniture.

MISS PEAKE. Oh yes, in Mr Sellon's time. You can't see him today, you know. He's dead.

OLIVER. No, I didn't come to see him. I came to see—(*with some emphasis*) Mrs Brown.

MISS PEAKE. Oh yes. Well, now you've seen her.

OLIVER (*turning his head to look at Clarissa*) Good-bye, Clarissa. You will hear from me, you know.

MISS PEAKE (*as she exits by the french windows*) This way, Mr Costello. Do you want the bus or did you bring your own?

OLIVER (*following Miss Peake*) I left my car round by the stables.

(MISS PEAKE *and* OLIVER *exit by the french windows*)

PIPPA. He'll take me away from here.

CLARISSA. No.

PIPPA. I hate him. I always hated him.

CLARISSA. Pippa!

PIPPA (*backing behind the armchair*) I don't want to go back to mother, I'd rather die. I'd much rather die. I'll kill him.

CLARISSA. Pippa!

PIPPA (*very hysterically*) I'll kill myself. I'll cut my wrists and bleed to death.

CLARISSA (*seizing her by the shoulders*) Pippa. Control yourself. It's all right, I tell you. *I'm* here.

PIPPA. I don't want to go back to mother and I hate Oliver. He's wicked, wicked, wicked.

CLARISSA. Yes, dear, I know. I know.

PIPPA (*hopefully*) Perhaps he'll be struck by lightning.

CLARISSA. Very likely. Now pull yourself together, Pippa. Everything's quite all right. (*She takes a handkerchief from her pocket*) Here, blow your nose.

(PIPPA *blows her nose, then wipes her tears off Clarissa's dress*)

(*She laughs*) You go and have your bath. (*She turns Pippa round to face the hall doors*) Mind you have a really good wash—your neck is absolutely filthy.

PIPPA (*becoming more normal*) It always is. (*She goes to the hall doors*)

(CLARISSA *moves above the left end of the sofa*)

(*She turns and runs to Clarissa. With a sudden rush of words*) You won't let him take me away, will you?

CLARISSA (*with determination*) Over my dead body—no. Over his dead body. There! Does that satisfy you?

(PIPPA *nods*)

(*She kisses Pippa's forehead*) Now, run along.

(PIPPA *hugs Clarissa then exits to the hall.* CLARISSA *switches on the concealed lighting by the switch above the hall door. She then crosses to the french windows, closes them, and flops down on to the right end of the sofa and puts her feet up. The front door is heard to slam off.*
HENRY HAILSHAM-BROWN *enters from the hall. He is a good-looking man of about forty with a rather expressionless face. He wears horn-rimmed spectacles and carries a brief-case*)

HENRY. Hullo, darling. (*He switches on the wall-brackets by the switch below the hall door and puts his brief-case in the armchair*)

CLARISSA. Hullo, Henry. Hasn't it been an awful day?

HENRY (*crossing behind the sofa*) Has it? (*He leans over the back of the sofa and kisses Clarissa*)

CLARISSA. Have a drink?

HENRY. Not just now. (*He moves to the french windows and closes the curtains*) Who's in the house? (*He moves towards the upstage window, but stops and turns when Clarissa speaks*)

CLARISSA (*surprised*) Nobody. It's the Elgins' night out. Black Thursday, you know. Cold ham, chocolate mousse——

(HENRY *crosses below the sofa to C*)

—and the coffee will be really good because *I* shall make it.

HENRY (*turning to her*) Um?

CLARISSA (*struck by his manner*) Henry, is anything the matter?

HENRY (*with a step towards her*) Well, yes, in a way.

CLARISSA. Something wrong? Miranda?

HENRY. No, no, nothing wrong. I should say quite the contrary. Yes, quite the contrary.

(CLARISSA *speaks with affection and very faint ridicule*)

CLARISSA. Darling, do I perceive behind the impenetrable Foreign Office façade a certain human excitement?

HENRY. Well, it is rather exciting in a way. (*He takes a step towards her*) As it happens there's a slight fog in London.

CLARISSA. Is that exciting?

HENRY. No, no, not the fog, of course.

CLARISSA. Well?

(HENRY *looks quickly around, then moves to the sofa and sits beside Clarissa*)

HENRY. You'll have to keep this to yourself, Clarissa.

CLARISSA (*hopefully*) Yes?

HENRY. It's really very secret. Nobody's supposed to know. Actually, you'll have to know.

CLARISSA. Well, come on, tell me.

(HENRY *again looks around then turns to Clarissa*)

HENRY. It's all very hush-hush. Kalendorff is flying to London for a conference tomorrow.

CLARISSA (*unimpressed*) Yes, I know.

HENRY (*startled*) What do you mean, you know?

CLARISSA. I read it in the paper last Sunday.

HENRY I can't think why you want to read these low-class papers. Anyway, the papers couldn't possibly know that Kalendorff was coming over. It's top secret.

CLARISSA. My poor sweet. Top secret indeed. The things you high-ups believe.

HENRY (*rising and crossing down* R; *worried*) Oh dear, there must have been some leak.

CLARISSA. I should have thought that by now you'd know there always *is* a leak. I should have thought you'd all be prepared for it.

HENRY. The news was only released officially tonight. Kalendorff's plane is due at Heath Row at eight forty, but actually . . . (*He leans over the end of the sofa and looks doubtfully at Clarissa*) Now, Clarissa, can I trust you to be discreet?

CLARISSA (*swinging her feet off the sofa and sitting up*) I'm much more discreet than any Sunday newspaper.

HENRY (*sitting on the right arm of the sofa*) The conference is tomorrow, but it would be a great advantage if a conversation could take place first between Sir John himself and Kalendorff. Now, naturally the reporters are all waiting at Heath Row and the moment the plane arrives, Kalendorff's movements are more or less public property. But fortunately, this incipient fog has played into our hands.

CLARISSA. Go on. I'm thrilled.

HENRY. The plane, at the last moment, will find it inadvisable to land at Heath Row. It will be diverted, as is usual on these occasions . . .

CLARISSA (*interrupting*) To Bindley Heath. That's just fifteen miles from here. I see.

HENRY. You're always very quick, Clarissa. Yes, I shall go off there now to the aerodrome in the car, meet Kalendorff and bring him here. Sir John is motoring down here directly from London. Twenty minutes will be ample for what they have to discuss, and Kalendorff will go back to London with Sir John. (*He hesitates, rises and crosses above the sofa to* C. *Suddenly rather disarming*) You know, Clarissa, this may be of very great value to me in my career. I mean, they're reposing a lot of trust in me having this meeting here.

CLARISSA. So they should. (*She rises, moves to Henry and flings her arms around him*) Henry, darling, I think it's all *wonderful.*

HENRY. By the way, Kalendorff will be referred to as Mr Jones.

CLARISSA. Mr Jones?

HENRY. One can't be too careful about using real names.

CLARISSA. Yes—but—Mr Jones. Couldn't they have thought of something better than *that?* What about me? Do I retire to the harem, as it were, or do I bring in the drinks, utter greetings and then discreetly fade away?

HENRY (*a little uneasily*) You must take this seriously, dear.

CLARISSA. But, Henry, darling, can't I take it seriously and still enjoy it a little?

HENRY (*considering*) I think it would be better, perhaps, Clarissa, if you didn't appear.

CLARISSA. All right. What about food? Will they want something?

HENRY. Oh no. There need be no question of a meal.

CLARISSA. A few sandwiches? (*She sits on the left arm of the sofa*) Ham sandwiches? In a napkin to keep them moist. Hot coffee, in a thermos jug. Yes, that'll do very well. The chocolate mousse I shall take up to my bedroom to console me for being excluded from the conference.

HENRY (*with a step towards her, disapprovingly*) Now, Clarissa.

CLARISSA (*rising and flinging her arms around his neck*) Darling, I am serious really. Nothing shall go wrong. I won't let it. (*She kisses Henry, then crosses below him to* LC)

HENRY. What about old Roly?

CLARISSA (*standing behind the armchair*) He and Jeremy are dining at the club house with Hugo. They're going to play bridge afterwards, so they won't be home till about midnight.

HENRY. And the Elgins are out?

CLARISSA. Darling, you know they always go to the cinema on Thursdays. They won't be back till after eleven.

HENRY. Good. That's all quite satisfactory. Sir John and Mr —er . . .

CLARISSA. Jones.

HENRY. Quite right, darling—will have left long before then. Well—(*he consults his watch*) I'd better have a quick wash before starting off for Bindley Heath.

CLARISSA. I'll go and make the ham sandwiches.

(CLARISSA *exits to the hall.* HENRY *picks up his brief-case*)

HENRY (*calling*) You must remember about the lights, Clarissa. (*He moves to the hall door and switches off the concealed lighting*) We're making our own electricity here. (*He switches off the wall-brackets*) Not like London.

(HENRY *exits to the hall, closing the door behind him. The room is in darkness except for faint moonlight coming in by the window up* R. OLIVER *enters stealthily by the french windows, leaving the curtain open so that the moonlight streams in. He plays an electric torch carefully around the room, then goes to the desk and switches on the desk lamp. He lifts the flap of the secret drawer, thinks he hears something, switches off the lamp and stands motionless for a moment. He switches on the desk lamp again, opens the secret drawer and takes out a slip of paper. The panel slowly opens. Without looking at the paper,* OLIVER *shuts the secret drawer, then hears something, turns sharply and switches off the desk light*)

OLIVER: What the . . .?

(*Somebody unseen behind the panel hits* OLIVER *on the head and he collapses behind the sofa. The panel closes. The moment Oliver is hit,* CLARISSA *is heard off*)

CLARISSA (*off, calling*) Henry! (*She pauses*) Henry, do you want a sandwich before you go?

(OLIVER *falls behind the sofa. There is a pause.*
HENRY *enters from the hall and switches on the wall-brackets. He crosses to* L *of the sofa and polishes his spectacles*)

HENRY (*shouting*) Clarissa! (*He puts on his spectacles, then fills his cigarette case with cigarettes from the box on the table* L *of the sofa*)

CLARISSA (*off, calling*) Here. Do you want a sandwich before you go?

HENRY (*shouting*) No. I think I'd better start.

CLARISSA. You'll be hours too early. It can't take you more than twenty minutes to drive there.

(CLARISSA *enters quietly from the hall and crosses to* L *of Henry*)

HENRY (*with his back to Clarissa; shouting*) One never knows. I might have a puncture or something might . . . (*He turns and sees Clarissa. In his normal voice*) Oh, there you are, darling. Something might go wrong with the car.

CLARISSA Don't fuss, darling.

HENRY. What about Pippa? She won't come down or barge in?

CLARISSA. No, I'll go up to the schoolroom and we'll have a feast together. We'll toast tomorrow's breakfast sausages and share the chocolate mousse between us.

HENRY. How very good you are to Pippa. It's one of the things I'm most grateful to you for. I never can express myself very well. (*Rather incoherently he goes on*) So much misery—and now—everything's so different. You . . . (*He kisses Clarissa*)

CLARISSA. You go and meet your Mr Jones. (*She pushes Henry towards the hall door*) I still think it's a ridiculous name to have chosen. Are you going to come in by the front door? Shall I leave it unlatched?

HENRY (*turning in the doorway*) No. I think we'd better use the window.

CLARISSA (*pushing Henry into the hall*) You'd better put on your overcoat, Henry, it's quite chilly.

(CLARISSA *and* HENRY *exit to the hall*)

(*Off*) And perhaps your muffler.

HENRY (*off*) Yes, dear.

CLARISSA (*off*) And drive carefully, darling, won't you?

HENRY (*off*) Yes, dear.

CLARISSA (*off*) Good-bye.

HENRY (*off*) Good-bye.

> (*The front door is heard to slam off.*
> CLARISSA *enters from the hall. She carries a plate of sandwiches wrapped in a napkin, which she puts on the table* L. *Then, remembering, she snatches the plate off, rubs at the mark, cannot move it and covers it with the vase of flowers. She crosses to the stool, puts the plate of sandwiches on the right end of it, then carefully shakes first the left and then the right cushions on the sofa. Humming to herself, she crosses to the table* LC, *picks up Pippa's book, moves up* C *and puts the book on the bookshelves*)

CLARISSA (*singing*) "Coming through the Rye. (*She turns and moves towards the desk*) Can a body meet a body, meet a body . . ." (*She does not get the last word out but screams as she nearly falls over Oliver's body. She bends over the body*) Oliver! (*She straightens up quickly and runs to* C, *to call for Henry, but realizes he has gone. She turns to the body again, then runs to the telephone, lifts the receiver, begins to dial, then stops and replaces the receiver. She moves* C *and stands thinking for a moment, then looks at the panel. She makes up her mind and moves behind the sofa. She looks at the panel again and then reluctantly she bends down and drags the body over*)

> (*The panel slowly opens.*
> PIPPA *enters from the recess. She wears a dressing-gown over her pyjamas*)

PIPPA (*crossing to* C) Clarissa!

CLARISSA (*trying to stand between Pippa and the body*) Pippa—(*she pushes Pippa a little* L *and tries to turn her away*) don't look. Don't look.

PIPPA (*in a strangled voice*) I didn't really mean to. Oh, really I didn't mean to do it.

CLARISSA (*seizing Pippa by her arms; horrified*) Pippa! Was it—you?

PIPPA. He's dead, isn't he? He's quite dead. (*Hysterically*) I didn't—mean to kill him. I didn't mean to. (*She sobs hysterically*) I didn't mean to.

CLARISSA. Quiet now, quiet. It's all right. Come, sit down. (*She leads Pippa to the armchair and sits her in it*)

PIPPA. I didn't mean to. I didn't mean to kill him.

CLARISSA (*kneeling beside her*) Of course you didn't mean to. Now listen, Pippa . . .

(PIPPA *cries even more hysterically*)

(*She shouts*) Pippa, listen to me. Everything's going to be all right. You've got to forget about this. Forget all about it, do you hear?

PIPPA. Yes. But—but I . . .

CLARISSA. Pippa, you must trust me and believe what I'm telling you. Everything is going to be all right. But you've got to be brave and do exactly what I tell you.

(PIPPA, *sobbing hysterically, turns away*)

Pippa! Will you do as I tell you? (*She pulls Pippa round*) Will you?

PIPPA. Yes, yes, I will. (*She puts her head on Clarissa's bosom*)

CLARISSA. That's right. (*She helps Pippa out of the chair*) I want you to go upstairs and get into bed.

PIPPA. You come with me.

CLARISSA (*leading Pippa towards the hall door*) Yes, yes, I'll come up very soon, as soon as I can, and I'll give you a nice little white tablet. Then you'll go to sleep and in the morning everything will seem quite different. (*She stops and looks towards the body*) There may be nothing to worry about.

PIPPA. But he is dead—isn't he? He is dead.

CLARISSA (*evasively*) No, no, he may not be dead. I'll see. Now go on, Pippa. Do as I tell you.

(PIPPA, *sobbing, exits by the hall door and goes up the stairs*)

(*She turns and crosses to* C) Supposing I were to find a dead body in the drawing-room, what should I do? What *am* I going to do?

CURTAIN

ACT II

SCENE I

SCENE—*The same. A quarter of an hour later.*
The easy chair is now down L, *the armchair is against the wall above the hall doors, and the small table* LC *is against the wall* L. *A folding bridge table is* LC *set out with cards and markers for bridge, with the four upright chairs around it.*
(See the Ground Plan at the end of the Play)

When the CURTAIN *rises the lights are on. The panel is closed and the curtains have been drawn over the open french windows. The body is still behind the sofa.* CLARISSA *is standing above the bridge table busily writing figures on one of the markers.*

CLARISSA (*muttering*) Three spades, four hearts, four no trumps, pass—(*she points at each hand as she makes its call*) five diamonds, pass, six spades—double—and I think they go down. Let me see, doubled vulnerable, two tricks, five hundred—or shall I let them make it? No.

(SIR ROWLAND, JEREMY *and* HUGO *enter by the french windows.* HUGO *pauses a moment and closes the upstage half of the french windows*)

(*She puts the pad and pencil on the bridge table and rushes down* L *of the sofa to meet Sir Rowland*) Thank God you've come.
SIR ROWLAND. What is all this, my dear?
CLARISSA. Darlings, you've got to help me.
JEREMY (*standing between the sofa and the stool, gaily*) Looks like a bridge party.
HUGO (*moving down* R *of Jeremy*) Melodramatics? What are you up to, young woman?
CLARISSA (*clutching Sir Rowland*) It's serious—terribly serious. You will help me, won't you?
SIR ROWLAND. Of course we'll help you, Clarissa, but what's it all about?
HUGO. What is this?
JEREMY (*unimpressed*) You're up to something, Clarissa. What is it? Found a body?
CLARISSA. That's just it. I have—found a body.
HUGO. What do you mean—found a body?
CLARISSA. It's just as Jeremy said. I came in here, and I found a body.
HUGO (*looking around*) Don't know what you're talking about.

27

CLARISSA. I'm serious. (*Angrily*) It is there. Go and look. Behind the sofa. (*She pushes Sir Rowland up* L *of the sofa and moves up* C)

(HUGO *moves quickly up* R *of the sofa.* JEREMY *leans over the back of the sofa and whistles*)

JEREMY. She's right. (*He moves to* R *of Hugo*)

(HUGO *and* SIR ROWLAND *bend down behind the sofa and look at the body*)

SIR ROWLAND. Why, it's Oliver Costello.

(JEREMY *quickly draws the curtains and moves to* R *of Hugo*)

CLARISSA. Yes.

SIR ROWLAND. What was he doing here?

CLARISSA. He came this evening to talk about Pippa—just after you'd gone to the club.

SIR ROWLAND. What did he want with Pippa?

CLARISSA. They were threatening to take her away. But all that doesn't matter now. We've got to hurry. We've very little time.

SIR ROWLAND. Just a moment. (*With a step towards Clarissa*) We must have the facts clear. What happened then?

CLARISSA. I told him that he wasn't having her and he went away.

SIR ROWLAND. But he came back?

CLARISSA. Obviously.

SIR ROWLAND. How? When?

CLARISSA. I don't know. I just came into the room as I said and found him—like that.

SIR ROWLAND (*moving to* L *of the body and leaning over it*) I see. Well, he's dead all right.

(CLARISSA *moves up* C *and stands with her back to the audience*)

Been hit over the head with something heavy and sharp. Well, it isn't going to be a very pleasant business—but there's only one thing to be done. (*He crosses to the telephone*) We must ring up the police . . .

CLARISSA (*turning*) No.

SIR ROWLAND (*lifting the receiver*) You ought to have done it at once, Clarissa. Still, they can't blame you much for that.

(CLARISSA *runs above Sir Rowland, takes the receiver from him and replaces it on the rest*)

CLARISSA. No, Roly, stop!

SIR ROWLAND. My dear child . . .

CLARISSA. I could have rung up the police myself if I'd wanted to. I knew perfectly well that it was the thing to do. I even started dialling. Then, instead, I rang *you* up. I asked you to come here, all three of you. (*She turns to Jeremy and Hugo*) You haven't even asked me why yet.

SIR ROWLAND. You can leave it all to us. We will . . .

CLARISSA (*turning to Sir Rowland*)   You haven't begun to understand. I want you to help me. You said you would if I was ever in trouble. (*She crosses above the bridge table to* C) Darlings, you've *got* to help me.

JEREMY (*moving above the table* L *of the sofa to hide the body from Clarissa*) What do you want us to do, Clarissa?

CLARISSA. Get rid of the body.

SIR ROWLAND (*moving to* L *of Clarissa*) My dear, don't talk nonsense. This is murder.

CLARISSA. That's the whole point. The body mustn't be found in this house.

HUGO (*crossing above Jeremy to* R *of Clarissa*) You don't know what you're talking about, my dear girl. You've been reading murder mysteries. In real life you can't go monkeying about moving dead bodies.

CLARISSA. I have moved it already. I turned it over to see if he were dead and then I started dragging it into that recess, and then I saw I'd got to have help, and so I rang you up, and whilst I was waiting for you I made a plan.

JEREMY (*moving below the left end of the sofa*) Including the bridge table?

CLARISSA (*picking up the bridge marker*) Yes, that's going to be our alibi.

HUGO. What on earth . . .?

CLARISSA. Two and a half rubbers. I've imagined all the hands and put down the scores on this marker. You three must fill up the others in your own handwriting of course.

SIR ROWLAND. You're mad, Clarissa—quite mad.

CLARISSA. I've worked it out beautifully. The body has to be taken away from here. (*She looks at Jeremy*) It will take two of you to do that. A dead body is terribly unmanageable—I've found that out already.

HUGO. Where the hell do you expect us to take it?

CLARISSA (*with a step towards Hugo*) The best place, I think, would be Marsden Wood. That's only two miles from here. (*She indicates the direction with her left hand*) You turn off to the left a few yards after you've left the front gate—it's a side road, hardly any traffic on it. (*She turns to Sir Rowland*) Just leave the car by the side of the road when you get into the wood. Then you walk back here.

JEREMY. Do you mean dump the body in the wood?

CLARISSA (*turning to Jeremy*) No, leave it in the car. It's *his* car, don't you see? He left it round by the stables. It's really all quite easy. If anybody does happen to see you walking back it's quite a dark night and they won't know who you are. And you've got an alibi. We have all four been playing bridge here. (*She replaces the marker on the bridge table*)

(*The others, stupefied, stare at Clarissa*)

HUGO (*moving up* c *and turning a complete circle*) I—I . . . (*He waves his hands*)

CLARISSA. You wear gloves, of course, so as not to leave finger-prints on anything. I've got them here all ready. (*She moves to Jeremy, pushes him below the sofa, takes three pairs of gloves from under the left cushion of the sofa and lays them out on the left arm of the sofa*)

SIR ROWLAND. Your natural talent for crime leaves me speech-less.

JEREMY (*admiringly*) She's got it all worked out, hasn't she?

HUGO (*moving to* L *of Clarissa*) Yes, but it's all damned fool nonsense, all the same.

CLARISSA (*vehemently*) But you must *hurry*. At nine o'clock, Henry and Mr Jones will be here.

SIR ROWLAND. Mr Jones? Who is Mr Jones?

CLARISSA (*putting her hand to her head*) Oh dear, I never realized what a terrible lot of explaining one has to do in a murder. I thought I'd ask you to help me and you would, and that is all there would be to it. Oh darlings, you must—you must—Hugo—(*she strokes Hugo's hair*) darling, darling, Hugo . . .

HUGO. Play acting's all very well, my dear—but a dead man's a nasty serious business—and monkeying about with it might land you in a real mess. You can't go carting bodies about at dead of night.

CLARISSA (*moving to* L *of Jeremy*) Jeremy?

JEREMY (*cheerfully*) I'm game. What's a dead body or two?

SIR ROWLAND (*moving down* L *of the bridge table*) Stop, young man. I'm not going to allow it. Clarissa, you've got to be guided by me. There's Henry to consider, too.

CLARISSA (*moving down* R *of the bridge table*) But it's Henry I *am* considering.

(HUGO *moves down* R)

Something terribly important is happening tonight. Henry's gone to—to meet someone and bring him back here. It's very impor-tant and secret. No-one was to know. There was to be absolutely no publicity.

SIR ROWLAND (*dubiously*) A Mr Jones.

CLARISSA. Silly name, I agree—but that's what they're calling him. I can't tell you about it. I promised I wouldn't say a word to anybody, but I have to make you see that I'm not just—(*she turns to look at Hugo*) being an idiot and play acting as Hugo called it. (*She turns to Sir Rowland*) What sort of effect do you think it will have on Henry's career to walk in here and find the police in charge of a murder, and the murder that of the man who has just married his former wife?

SIR ROWLAND. Good Lord! (*Suspiciously*) You're not making all this up, Clarissa?

CLARISSA. Nobody ever believes me when I'm speaking the truth.

SIR ROWLAND. Sorry. (*Thoughtfully*) Yes, it's a more difficult problem than I thought.

CLARISSA. You see? We must get the body away from here.

JEREMY. Where's his car, do you say?

CLARISSA (*with a step towards Jeremy*) Round by the stables.

JEREMY. And the servants are out, I gather.

CLARISSA. Yes.

JEREMY (*picking up a pair of gloves*) Right. Do I take the body to the car or the car to the body?

SIR ROWLAND. Wait a moment. We mustn't rush it like this.

(JEREMY *replaces the gloves*)

CLARISSA (*turning to Sir Rowland*) But we must *hurry*.

SIR ROWLAND (*with a step towards Clarissa*) I'm not sure that this plan of yours is the best one, Clarissa. Now, if we could just delay finding the body until tomorrow morning—that would meet the case, I think, and be very much simpler. If we merely moved the body to another room, for instance, that might be just excusable.

CLARISSA (*moving to R of Sir Rowland*) It's *you* I've got to convince, isn't it? (*She looks at Jeremy*) Jeremy's ready enough—(*she looks at Hugo*) and Hugo will grunt and shake his head and growl—(*she turns to Sir Rowland*) but he'd do it all the same. It's you . . . (*She moves to the library door and opens it*) Will you both go next door for a short time? I want to speak to Roly alone.

(SIR ROWLAND *sits on the chair* L *of the bridge table*)

HUGO (*crossing to the library door; to Sir Rowland*) Don't you let her talk you into any tomfoolery, Roly.

JEREMY (*crossing to the library door; to Clarissa*) Good luck!

(HUGO *and* JEREMY *exit to the library*. CLARISSA *closes the door*)

CLARISSA. Now! (*She moves to the chair* R *of the bridge table and sits*)

SIR ROWLAND. My dear, I love you, and will always love you dearly, but in this case, the answer is no.

CLARISSA (*seriously, and with emphasis*) That man's body mustn't be found in this house. If he's found in Marsden Wood, I can say that he was here today for a short time, and I can also tell the police exactly when he left—actually Miss Peake saw him off, which turns out to be very fortunate. There need be no question of his ever having come back here. But if his body is found *here*, then we shall all be questioned—(*with deliberation*) and Pippa won't be able to stand it.

SIR ROWLAND (*puzzled*) Pippa?

CLARISSA. She'll break down and confess.

SIR ROWLAND (*taking it in*) Pippa!

(CLARISSA *nods*)

My God!

CLARISSA. She was terrified when he came here today. I told her I wouldn't let her be taken away but I don't think she believed me. You know what she's been through—the nervous breakdown she's had? She told me she never meant to do it, and that's true, I'm sure. It was panic. She got hold of that stick and struck out blindly.

SIR ROWLAND. What stick?

CLARISSA. The one from the hall stand. It's in the recess. I left it there, I didn't touch it.

SIR ROLAND (*sharply*) Where is she now?

CLARISSA. In bed. I've given her a sleeping pill. She ought not to wake till morning. Tomorrow I'll take her up to London— my old nanny will look after her.

(SIR ROWLAND *rises, crosses below the bridge table to* L *of the body, glances at it, then returns to Clarissa and kisses her*)

SIR ROWLAND. You win, my dear. I apologize. That child mustn't be asked to face the music. Get the others. (*He crosses quickly to the french windows, looks out, then closes the curtains*)

(CLARISSA *rises, goes to the library door and opens it*)

CLARISSA (*calling*) Hugo. Jeremy. (*She moves above the bridge table*)

(HUGO *and* JEREMY *enter from the library*)

HUGO. That butler of yours doesn't lock up very carefully. The window in the library was open. I've shut it now. (*To Sir Rowland*) Well?

SIR ROWLAND (*moving down* R *of the sofa*) I'm converted.

JEREMY (*moving to* R *of Clarissa*) Well done.

SIR ROWLAND (*moving above the sofa*) There's no time to lose. Those gloves. (*He picks up a pair of gloves and puts them on*)

(JEREMY *picks up two pairs of gloves, hands one pair to Hugo and puts the other pair on.* HUGO *puts on the gloves*)

(*He moves to the panel*) Now how does this thing open?

JEREMY (*moving up* C) Like this, sir, Pippa showed me. (*He moves the lever and opens the panel*)

(SIR ROWLAND *looks into the recess and brings out the knobkerry*)

SIR ROWLAND. Heavy enough. Weighted in the head. All the same, I shouldn't have thought . . .

HUGO. What wouldn't you have thought?

SIR ROWLAND. I should have thought it would have been something with a sharper edge—metal of some kind.

HUGO. You mean a God-damned chopper?

JEREMY. That stick looks pretty murderous to me. You could easily crack a man's head open with that.

SIR ROWLAND. Evidently. Hugo, will you burn this in the kitchen stove. (*He hands the knobkerry to Hugo*) Warrender, you and I'll get the body to the car. (*He bends down R of the body*)

(JEREMY *bends down* L *of the body. The front door bell peals suddenly off.* JEREMY *and* SIR ROWLAND *straighten up*)

What's that?

CLARISSA (*bewildered*) It's the front door bell.

(*They all stand petrified*)

Who can it be? It's much too early for Henry and Mr Jones. It must be Sir John.

SIR ROWLAND. Sir John? You mean the Foreign Secretary?

CLARISSA. Yes.

SIR ROWLAND. Hm—yes. Well, we've got to do something.

(*The bell rings again*)

Clarissa, go and answer the door. Use what delaying tactics you can. In the meantime, we'll clear up in here.

(CLARISSA *exits to the hall*)

Now then, we'll get him in here. Later, when everyone's in here at the pow-wow, we can take him out through the library.

JEREMY. Good idea.

(JEREMY *and* SIR ROWLAND *lift the body*)

HUGO. Give you a hand?

JEREMY. No. It's all right.

(JEREMY *and* SIR ROWLAND *support the body under the armpits and carry it into the recess.* HUGO *picks up the torch.* SIR ROWLAND *comes out of the recess and presses the lever, as* JEREMY *slips out.* HUGO *slips under* Jeremy's *arm into the recess with the torch and stick. The panel closes*)

SIR ROWLAND (*looking at his coat for blood*) Gloves. (*He removes the gloves and puts them under the cushion at the left end of the sofa*)

(JEREMY *removes his gloves and puts them under the cushion*)

Bridge. (*He moves to the bridge table and sits above it*)

(JEREMY *runs to* L *of the bridge table, turns over the downstage hand and picks up his own cards*)

(*He picks up his cards*) Come along, Hugo.

(HUGO *knocks from inside the recess.* JEREMY *and* SIR ROWLAND *realize that Hugo is not there, and look at each other.* JEREMY *rises, rushes to the switch and opens the panel.* SIR ROWLAND *rises and crosses to* R *of the panel.* HUGO *comes out of the recess*)

Come along, Hugo.

JEREMY (*closing the panel*)　Hurry up, Hugo.

(SIR ROWLAND *takes Hugo's gloves and puts them under the cushion. They all run to their seats:* HUGO, R *of the table,* SIR ROWLAND *above it, and* JEREMY L *of it. They pick up their cards.*

CLARISSA, INSPECTOR LORD *and* CONSTABLE JONES *enter from the hall*)

CLARISSA (*all surprise*)　It's the police, Uncle Roly. (*She stands behind Sir Rowland's chair*)

(*The* CONSTABLE *stands by the hall doors*)

INSPECTOR (*moving to* L *of Clarissa*)　I'm sorry to intrude, gentlemen, but we have received information that a murder has been committed here.

HUGO			What!
JEREMY			A murder!
SIR ROWLAND	}	(*together*)	What!
CLARISSA			Isn't it extraordinary?

INSPECTOR.　We had a telephone call at the station. (*To Hugo*) Good evening, Mr Birch.

HUGO (*mumbling*)　Er—good evening, Inspector.

SIR ROWLAND.　It looks as though somebody's been hoaxing you, Inspector.

CLARISSA.　We've been playing bridge here all evening.

(*The others nod agreement*)

Who did they say had been murdered?

INSPECTOR.　No names were mentioned. The caller just said that a man had been murdered at Copplestone Court and would we come along immediately. They rang off before any additional information could be obtained.

CLARISSA.　It must have been a hoax. (*Virtuously*) What a wicked thing to do.

(HUGO "*tut-tuts*")

INSPECTOR.　You'd be surprised, madam, at the potty things people do do.

(HUGO *clears his throat, rises, crosses and sits on the left arm of the sofa*)

Well now, according to you, nothing out of the ordinary has happened here this evening? Perhaps I'd better see Mr Hailsham-Brown as well.

CLARISSA (*moving* C) He's not here. I don't expect him back until late tonight.

INSPECTOR (*moving to* L *of Clarissa*) I see. Who is there in the house?

CLARISSA (*indicating them in turn*) Sir Rowland Delahaye. Mr Warrender.

(SIR ROWLAND *and* JEREMY *murmur acknowledgements*)

And my *little* step-daughter. She's in bed and asleep.

INSPECTOR. What about servants?

CLARISSA. It's their night out. They're at the pictures in Maidstone.

INSPECTOR. I see.

(ELGIN *enters from the hall*)

ELGIN (*standing above Jeremy and looking at the Inspector*) Would you be wanting anything, madam?

CLARISSA (*startled*) I thought you were at the pictures, Elgin?

(*The* INSPECTOR *looks sharply at Clarissa*)

ELGIN. We returned almost immediately, madam. My wife was not feeling well—(*delicately*) er—gastric trouble. (*He looks from the Inspector to the Constable*) Is anything—wrong?

INSPECTOR. What's your name?

ELGIN. Elgin. I'm sure I hope there's nothing . . .

INSPECTOR. Someone rang up the station and said that a murder had been committed here.

ELGIN. A murder?

INSPECTOR. What do you know about that?

ELGIN. Nothing, nothing at all.

(CLARISSA *crosses and stands above the right end of the sofa*)

INSPECTOR. It wasn't you who rang up?

ELGIN. No, indeed.

INSPECTOR. You came in by the back door—(*he takes a step* R *then turns to Elgin*) I suppose?

ELGIN. Yes, sir.

INSPECTOR. Notice anything unusual?

ELGIN (*with a step towards the Inspector*) Now I think of it, there was a strange car standing near the stables.

INSPECTOR. A strange car?

ELGIN. I wondered at the time whose it might be. It seemed a curious place to leave it.

INSPECTOR. Anybody in it?

ELGIN. Not so far as I could see, sir.

INSPECTOR (*to the Constable*) Go and take a look at it, Jones.

CLARISSA (*looking out front; startled*) Jones!

INSPECTOR (*turning to Clarissa*) I beg your pardon?

CLARISSA (*turning and smiling at the Inspector*) Nothing—just—I didn't think he looked very Welsh.

(*The* INSPECTOR *signs to the Constable and Elgin, indicating they should go.*

ELGIN *and the* CONSTABLE *exit to the hall, closing the door.* JEREMY *rises and crosses to the sofa, sits on it at the right end, and eats the sandwiches. The* INSPECTOR *puts his hat and gloves on the armchair, then moves to* L *of the bridge table*)

INSPECTOR. It seems that someone called here tonight who is unaccounted for. You weren't expecting anyone?

CLARISSA (*moving* C) Oh, no—no. We didn't want anyone. You see, we were just the four of us for bridge.

INSPECTOR. Oh, I'm fond of a game of bridge myself.

CLARISSA (*moving up* R *of Sir Rowland*) Oh, are you? Do you play Blackwood?

INSPECTOR (*moving below the table*) I just like a common-sense game. (*He crosses to* R *of Clarissa*) You haven't been here very long, have you, Mrs Hailsham-Brown?

CLARISSA (*moving above Sir Rowland to* L *of him*) No, about six weeks.

INSPECTOR. And there's been no funny business of any kind since you've been here?

SIR ROWLAND. What exactly do you mean by funny business, Inspector?

INSPECTOR. Well, it's rather a curious story, sir. This house belonged to Mr Sellon the antique dealer. He died six months ago.

CLARISSA. Yes, he had some kind of accident, didn't he?

INSPECTOR. That's right. Fell downstairs, pitched on his head. (*He looks at Jeremy*) Accidental death, they brought in. Might have been that, might not.

CLARISSA. You mean, somebody might have pushed him?

INSPECTOR (*turning to Clarissa*) That, or else somebody hit him a crack on the head——

(HUGO *rises, moves to the desk stool and sits. The others freeze*)

(*He turns to Jeremy*)—and arranged him to look right at the bottom of the stairs.

CLARISSA. These stairs here?

INSPECTOR (*turning to Clarissa*) No, at the shop. No evidence, of course—but he was rather a dark horse, Mr Sellon.

SIR ROWLAND. In what way, Inspector?

INSPECTOR. Once or twice he had a couple of things to explain, as you might say. And the Narcotic Squad came down and had a word with him once—(*he turns to Jeremy*) but it was all only suspicion.

SIR ROWLAND. Officially, that is to say.

INSPECTOR (*turning to Sir Rowland*) That's right, sir, officially.

SIR ROWLAND. Whereas unofficially . . .?

INSPECTOR. I'm afraid we can't mention that. (*He turns to Jeremy*) But there was one rather curious circumstance. There was an unfinished letter on Mr Sellon's desk, in which he mentioned that he'd come into possession of something which he described as an unparalleled rarity, which he would—(*he turns to Sir Rowland*) guarantee wasn't a forgery and he was asking fourteen thousand pounds for it.

SIR ROWLAND. Fourteen thousand pounds, that's a lot of money. I wonder what it could be? Jewellery, I suppose, but the word forgery . . . A picture, perhaps?

(JEREMY *continues to eat the sandwiches*)

INSPECTOR. Yes. There was nothing in the shop worth such a sum of money. The Insurance inventory made that clear. (*He turns to Jeremy*) Mr Sellon's partner was a woman who has a business on her own in London, and she wrote and said she couldn't give us any help.

SIR ROWLAND. So he might have been murdered and the article, whatever it was, stolen.

INSPECTOR (*turning to Sir Rowland*) It's possible, but again the would-be thief mayn't have been able to find it.

SIR ROWLAND. Now why do you think that?

INSPECTOR. Because the shop has been broken into twice since then—(*he turns to Jeremy*) broken into and ransacked.

CLARISSA. Why are you telling us all this, Inspector?

INSPECTOR (*turning to Clarissa*) Because, Mrs Hailsham-Brown, it's occurred to me that whatever was hidden away by Sellon may have been hidden *here*, and not at the shop in Maidstone, and that's why I asked you if anything peculiar had come to your notice.

CLARISSA. Somebody rang up today and asked to speak to me, and when I came to the phone, whoever it was—just hung up. In a way, that's rather odd. Oh yes, of course—(*to Jeremy*) that man who came the other day and wanted to buy things—a horsey sort of man in a check suit. He wanted to buy that desk.

INSPECTOR (*crossing and standing up L of the desk*) This one here?

(HUGO *rises*)

CLARISSA (*crossing to L of the Inspector*) Yes. I told him, of course, that it wasn't ours to sell but he didn't seem to believe me. He offered a large sum, far more than it's worth.

INSPECTOR. Interesting. (*He studies the desk*) These things often have a secret drawer.

CLARISSA. Yes, this one has. But there was nothing very exciting in it: only some old autographs.

(*The* CONSTABLE *enters from the hall. He carries a car registration book and a pair of gloves. He stands just inside the doorway*)

INSPECTOR (*crossing to the Constable*) Yes, Jones?
CONSTABLE (*with a Welsh accent*) I've examined the car, sir. Pair of gloves in the driving seat. Registration book in the side pocket. (*He hands the book to the Inspector*)

(CLARISSA *and* JEREMY *smile at each other when they hear the Constable's accent*)

INSPECTOR (*examining the book*) Oliver Costello, twenty-seven, Morgan Mansions, S.W. Three. (*He moves to* L *of the bridge table. Sharply*) Has a man called Costello been here today?

(CLARISSA *and* SIR ROWLAND *exchange a quick glance*)

CLARISSA (*moving* C) Yes, he was here about—let me see—half past six.
INSPECTOR. A friend of yours?
CLARISSA. No. I shouldn't call him a friend. I had met him once or twice. (*Deliberately looking embarrassed*) It's—a little awkward . . . (*She passes the ball to Sir Rowland*)
SIR ROWLAND. Perhaps it would be better if I explained the situation, Inspector. It concerns the first Mrs Hailsham-Brown. There was a divorce just over a year ago, and recently she married Mr Oliver Costello.
INSPECTOR. I see. And Mr Costello came here today—why? By appointment?
CLARISSA (*easily*) Oh, no. As a matter of fact, when Miranda left she took with her one or two things that weren't really hers. Oliver happened to be in this part of the world and he just looked in to return them.
INSPECTOR. What kind of things?
CLARISSA (*smiling*) Nothing very important. (*She picks up the small silver cigarette box from the table* L *of the sofa*) This was one of them. (*She moves to* R *of the card table and shows the box to the Inspector*) It belonged to my husband's mother and he values it for sentimental reasons.
INSPECTOR. How long did Mr Costello remain?
CLARISSA (*replacing the box on the table* L *of the sofa*) Oh, a very short time. He said he was in a hurry. About ten minutes, I should think.
INSPECTOR (*crossing above the bridge table to* L *of Clarissa*) And your interview was quite amicable?
CLARISSA. Oh, yes. I thought it was very kind of him to take the trouble to return the things.

INSPECTOR. Did he mention where he was going when he left here?

CLARISSA. No, actually he went out by that window. As a matter of fact, my lady gardener, Miss Peake, was here and she *offered* to show him out through the garden.

INSPECTOR. Your gardener. Does she live on the premises?

CLARISSA. Yes, she lives in the cottage.

INSPECTOR. I think I should like a word with her. Jones!

CLARISSA. There's a telephone connexion through to the cottage. Shall I get her for you, Inspector? (*She crosses below the card table to the telephone and lifts the receiver*)

INSPECTOR. If you would be so kind, Mrs Hailsham-Brown.

(HUGO *moves to the upstage end of the desk*)

CLARISSA. Oh, not at all. (*She presses a knob on the telephone*) I don't suppose she'll have gone to bed yet. (*She smiles at the Inspector*)

(*The* INSPECTOR *looks bashful.* JEREMY *smiles and takes another sandwich*)

(*Into the telephone*) Hullo, Miss Peake. This is Mrs Hailsham-Brown . . . Would you mind coming over? Something rather important has happened . . . Oh yes, that will be all right, thank you. (*She replaces the receiver*) She's been washing her hair but she'll dress and come right over.

INSPECTOR. Thank you.

(CLARISSA *moves down* L)

He may have mentioned to her where he was going.

CLARISSA. Yes, he may have. (*She starts to cross to* R)

INSPECTOR (*moving down* C) The question is, why is Mr Costello's car still here, and where is Mr Costello?

(CLARISSA *momentarily stops, glances at the panel, then continues to the french windows. As Clarissa stops,* JEREMY *sits back innocently and crosses his legs*)

Apparently Miss Peake was the last person to see him. He left, you say, by that window. Did you lock it after him?

CLARISSA (*standing at the window with her back to the Inspector*) No.

INSPECTOR. Oh.

CLARISSA (*turning to the Inspector*) I—I don't think so.

INSPECTOR. So he *might* have re-entered that way. I think, Mrs Hailsham-Brown, that with your permission, I should like to search the house.

CLARISSA (*smiling*) Of course. You've seen this room. Nobody could be hidden here. (*She holds the window curtains open for a moment*) Look! (*She crosses to the library door and opens it*) Through here is the library. Would you like to go in there?

INSPECTOR. Thank you. Jones!

(*The* INSPECTOR *and the* CONSTABLE *go into the library*)

(*As he goes; indicating the door* L *of the library backing*) Just see where that door leads to, Jones.

CONSTABLE (*off, opening the door*) Very good, sir.

(SIR ROWLAND *rises and runs to* R *of the panel*)

SIR ROWLAND (*gesticulating*) What's the other side?
CLARISSA. Bookshelves.

(SIR ROWLAND *nods and moves above the left end of the sofa*)

CONSTABLE (*off*) Just through to the hall, sir.

(*The* INSPECTOR *and the* CONSTABLE *enter from the library*)

INSPECTOR. Right. (*He notices that Sir Rowland has moved*) Now we'll search the rest of the house. (*He moves to the hall door*)
CLARISSA (*moving to* R *of the Inspector*) I'll come with you if you don't mind, in case my step-daughter should wake up and be frightened. Not that I think she will. It's extraordinary how deeply children sleep. You have fairly to shake them awake.

(*The* INSPECTOR *opens the hall doors*)

Have you got any children, Inspector?
INSPECTOR (*turning to Clarissa*) Boy and girl.

(*The* INSPECTOR *exits and goes up the stairs*)

CLARISSA. Isn't that nice. (*She turns to the Constable*) Mr Jones.

(*The* CONSTABLE *exits to the hall.* CLARISSA *follows him off, her smile dropping as she shuts the doors.* HUGO *wipes his hands and* JEREMY *mops his forehead*)

JEREMY. And now what? (*He takes another sandwich*)
SIR ROWLAND. I don't like this. We're getting in deep.
HUGO (*moving above the right end of the sofa*) If you ask me, there's only one thing to do, come clean. Own up now before it's too late.
JEREMY. Damn it, we can't do that. It would be too unfair to Clarissa.
HUGO. We'll get her in a worse mess if we keep on with this. How are we ever going to get the body away? The police will impound the fellow's car.
JEREMY. We'll use mine.
HUGO (*crossing above the sofa to* L *of Sir Rowland*) Well, I don't like it. I don't like it at all. Damn it, I'm a local J.P. What do you say, Roly? You've got a good level head.
SIR ROWLAND. Personally, I am committed to the enterprise.
HUGO (*moving to* R *of the bridge table*) I don't understand you.

SIR ROWLAND. Take it on trust, if you will. We're in a very bad jam, all of us. But if we stick together and have reasonable luck, I think there's a chance we may pull it off. Once the police are satisfied that Costello isn't in this house, they'll go off and look elsewhere. Plenty of reasons, you know, why he might have left his car and gone off on foot. I don't see why suspicion should attach itself to any of us. We're all respectable people—Hugo's a J.P. Henry's in the Foreign Office.

HUGO. And I suppose you've had a blameless and even distinguished career. All right then, we brazen it out.

JEREMY (*rising and moving, above the sofa*) Can't we do something about that straight away? (*He nods towards the recess*)

SIR ROWLAND. No time. They'll be back any minute. Safer where it is.

JEREMY. I must say Clarissa's a marvel. Doesn't turn a hair. She's got that police inspector eating out of her hand.

(*The front door bell rings off*)

SIR ROWLAND. That's Miss Peake, I expect. Go and let her in, Warrender.

(JEREMY *crosses and exits to the hall.* HUGO *beckons to* SIR ROWLAND, *who moves to him,* C)

HUGO. Roly—what's up, Roly? What did that girl tell you when she got you to herself?

JEREMY (*off*) Good evening, Miss Peake.

(SIR ROWLAND *starts to speak, but on hearing Miss Peake's voice, he indicates* "not now")

MISS PEAKE (*off*) Good evening, Mr Warrender.

(*The front door is heard to slam*)

JEREMY (*off*) I think you'd better come in here.

(JEREMY *and* MISS PEAKE *enter from the hall.* MISS PEAKE *is rather hastily dressed and has a towel around her head*)

MISS PEAKE. What is all this? Mrs Brown-Hailsham was most mysterious on the phone. Has anything happened?

SIR ROWLAND (*very courteously*) I'm so sorry you've been routed out like this, Miss Peake. (*He indicates the chair above the bridge table*) Do sit down.

(HUGO *pulls out the chair for Miss Peake, then sits in the easy chair down* L)

MISS PEAKE (*sitting above the bridge table*) Oh, thank you.

SIR ROWLAND. As a matter of fact we've got the police here, and . . .

MISS PEAKE. The police? Has there been a burglary?

SIR ROWLAND. No, not that—but . . .

(CLARISSA, *the* INSPECTOR *and the* CONSTABLE *enter from the hall.* SIR ROWLAND *backs above the sofa.* JEREMY *crosses and sits on the sofa*)

CLARISSA (*moving to* L *of Miss Peake*) Inspector, this is Miss Peake.

INSPECTOR (*moving to* R *of Miss Peake*) Good evening, Miss Peake.

MISS PEAKE. Good evening, Inspector. I was just asking Sir Rowland—has there been a robbery, or what?

INSPECTOR. We received a rather peculiar telephone call which brought us out here and we think you could probably clear up the matter for us.

(SIR ROWLAND *sits on the back of the sofa*)

MISS PEAKE (*with a jolly laugh*) This is mysterious.

INSPECTOR. It concerns Mr Costello, Mr Oliver Costello of twenty-seven Morgan Mansions, Chelsea.

MISS PEAKE. Never heard of him.

INSPECTOR. He was here this evening, visiting Mrs Hailsham-Brown, and I believe you showed him out through the garden.

MISS PEAKE. Oh, that man. Mrs Hailsham-Brown did mention his name. Yes, what do you want to know?

INSPECTOR. I should like to know exactly what happened, and when you last saw him.

MISS PEAKE. Let me see, we went out through the window, and I said there was a short cut if he wanted the bus, and he said no, he'd come in his car, and he'd left it round by the stables.

INSPECTOR. Rather an odd place to leave a car.

MISS PEAKE (*slapping the Inspector's arm*) Just what I thought.

(*The* INSPECTOR *looks surprised*)

You'd think he'd drive right up to the front door, wouldn't you? People are so odd.

INSPECTOR. And then?

MISS PEAKE. He went off to his car and I suppose he drove away.

INSPECTOR. You didn't see him do so?

MISS PEAKE. No—I was putting my tools away.

INSPECTOR. And that's the last you saw of him?

MISS PEAKE. Yes, why?

INSPECTOR. His car is still here. A call was put through to the police station at seven forty-nine, saying a man had been murdered at Copplestone Court.

MISS PEAKE. Murdered? Here? Ridiculous!

INSPECTOR. That's what everybody seems to think. (*He looks at Sir Rowland*)

MISS PEAKE. Of course I know there are all these maniacs about, attacking women—but you say a *man* was murdered . . .

INSPECTOR. You didn't hear a car this evening?

MISS PEAKE. Only Mr Hailsham-Brown's.

INSPECTOR. Mr Hailsham-Brown? I thought he wasn't expected home until late. (*His glance swings to Clarissa*)

CLARISSA. My husband did come home, but he had to go out again almost immediately.

INSPECTOR. Oh, is that so? Exactly when did he come home?

CLARISSA. Let me see—about . . .

MISS PEAKE. It was about quarter of an hour before I went off duty—I work a lot of overtime, Inspector. I never stick to regulation hours. Be keen on your job—(*she thumps the table*) that's what I say. Yes, it was about a quarter past seven when Mr Hailsham-Brown got in.

INSPECTOR (*moving* C) Shortly after Mr Costello left. (*His manner imperceptibly changes*) They probably passed each other.

MISS PEAKE. You mean that he may have come back again to see Mr Hailsham-Brown.

CLARISSA. Oliver definitely *didn't* come back to the house.

MISS PEAKE. But you can't be sure of that, Mrs Hailsham-Brown. He might have got in by that window without your knowing anything about it. Golly! You don't think he *murdered* Mr Hailsham-Brown? I say. I am sorry.

CLARISSA. Of course he didn't murder Henry.

INSPECTOR. Where did your husband go when he left here?

CLARISSA. I've no idea.

INSPECTOR. Doesn't he usually say where he's going?

CLARISSA. I never ask questions. I think it must be so boring for a man if his wife is always asking questions.

(MISS PEAKE *gives a sudden squeal*)

MISS PEAKE. But how stupid of me. Of course, if that man's car is still here, then *he* must be the one who's been murdered. (*She roars with laughter*)

SIR ROWLAND (*rising*) We've no reason to believe anyone has been murdered, Miss Peake. In fact, the Inspector believes it was all some silly hoax.

MISS PEAKE. But the car. I do think the car is very suspicious. (*She rises and moves to* L *of the Inspector*) Have you looked about for the body, Inspector?

SIR ROWLAND. The Inspector has already searched the house.

(*The* INSPECTOR *looks at Sir Rowland*)

MISS PEAKE (*tapping the Inspector on the shoulder*) I'm sure those Elgins have something to do with it. I've had my suspicions of them all along. I saw a light in their bedroom window as I came along here just now. And that in itself is suspicious. It's their night out and they usually don't return until past eleven. Have you searched their quarters?

(*The* INSPECTOR *opens his mouth to speak*)

(*She taps the Inspector on the shoulder*) Now, listen. Suppose this Mr Costello recognized Elgin as a man with a criminal record. He might decide to come back and warn Mrs Hailsham-Brown about the man, and Elgin assaulted him. Then, of course, Elgin would have to hide the body somewhere quickly, so that he could dispose of it later in the night. Now, where would he hide it, I wonder. (*She indicates the french windows*) Behind a curtain or . . .

CLARISSA. Oh, really, Miss Peake, there isn't anybody hidden behind any of the curtains. And I'm sure Elgin would never murder anybody. It's quite ridiculous.

MISS PEAKE (*turning and taking a step towards Clarissa*) You're so trusting, Mrs Hailsham-Brown. When you're my age, you'll realize how often people are not quite what they seem. (*She laughs and turns to the Inspector*)

(*The* INSPECTOR *opens his mouth to speak*)

(*She taps the Inspector on the shoulder*) Now then, where would a man like Elgin hide the body? There's that cupboard place between here and the library. You've looked there, I suppose?

SIR ROWLAND. Miss Peake, the Inspector has looked both——

(*The* INSPECTOR *looks at Sir Rowland*)

—here and in the library.

INSPECTOR (*turning to Miss Peake*) What do you mean by "that cupboard place", Miss Peake.

(*The others give a definite though controlled reaction*)

MISS PEAKE. Oh, it's a wonderful place when you're playing sardines. You'd really never dream it was there. I'll show it to you. (*She crosses above the Inspector to the panel*)

(*The* INSPECTOR *follows Miss Peake.* JEREMY *rises*)

CLARISSA. No.

(*The* INSPECTOR *and* MISS PEAKE *turn to Clarissa*)

(*She crosses to* L *of the Inspector*) There's nothing there now. I know because I went that way, through to the library, just now. (*Her voice trails off*)

MISS PEAKE (*disappointed*) Oh well, in that case, then . . . (*She turns away from the panel*)

(CLARISSA *moves down* C)

INSPECTOR (*moving to* L *of Miss Peake*) Just show me all the same. I'd like to see.

Miss Peake (*moving to the bookshelves up* c) It was a door originally—matched the one over there. (*She actuates the lever*) You pull this catch back, and the door comes open. You see.

(*The panel opens. The body slumps down and falls forward.* Miss Peake *screams*)

Inspector (*looking at Clarissa*) So there was a murder here tonight.

Miss Peake *continues to scream as the lights* Black-Out, *and—*

the Curtain *falls*

SCENE 2

Scene—*The same. Ten minutes later.*

When the Curtain *rises, the body is lying collapsed in the recess, the panel of which is open.* Clarissa *is lying on the sofa, with her head at the left end.* Sir Rowland *is sitting on the sofa, at the right end, holding a glass of brandy, which he is making* Clarissa *sip. The* Inspector *is talking on the telephone. The* Constable *is standing below the table up* c. *The chair below the bridge table is now* l *of the table up* c)

Inspector (*into the telephone*) Yes, yes . . . What's that? . . . Hit and run? . . . Where? . . . Oh, I see . . . Yes, well, send them along as soon as you can . . . Yes, we'll want photographs . . . Yes, the whole bag of tricks. (*He replaces the receiver and crosses to the Constable*) Everything comes at once. Weeks go by and nothing happens, now the Divisional Surgeon's out at a smash on the London road. It'll all mean a bit of delay. (*He crosses and stands below the recess*)

(*The* Constable *moves to* l *of the Inspector*)

However, we'll get on as best we can until the M.O. arrives. Better not move him until they've taken the photographs—not that it will tell us anything, he wasn't killed there. He was put there afterwards. (*He looks down at the carpet*) You can see where his feet have dragged. (*He crouches down behind the sofa*)

(*The* Constable *crouches down behind the sofa.* Sir Rowland *peers over the back of the sofa, then turns to Clarissa*)

Sir Rowland. How are you feeling?
Clarissa (*faintly*) Better.

(*The* Inspector *and the* Constable *rise*)

Inspector (*to the Constable*) Might be as well to close the book-case door, we don't want any more hysterics.

CONSTABLE. Right, sir. (*He closes the panel on the body in the recess*)

SIR ROWLAND (*rising, putting his glass on the table* R *of the sofa and moving round to* R *of the Inspector*) Mrs Hailsham-Brown has had a bad shock. I think she ought to go to her room and lie down.

INSPECTOR (*politely, but with a certain reserve*) Certainly, in a moment or two. I'd just like to ask her a few questions first.

SIR ROWLAND. She's not fit to be questioned.

CLARISSA (*faintly*) I'm all right. Really, I am.

SIR ROWLAND (*warningly*) It's very brave of you, my dear. But I really think it's wiser not.

CLARISSA. Dear Uncle Roly. (*To the Inspector*) He's so sweet to me always.

INSPECTOR. Yes, I can see that.

CLARISSA. Do ask me anything you want to, Inspector. Though actually I can't help you, I'm afraid, because I just don't know anything at all.

(SIR ROWLAND *sighs, shakes his head slightly, and turns away*)

INSPECTOR. We shan't worry you much, madam. (*He moves to the library door and opens it. To Sir Rowland*) Will you join the other gentlemen, sir?

SIR ROWLAND. I think I'd better remain here in case . . .

INSPECTOR (*firmly*) I'll call you if it should be necessary.

(*There is a slight duel of eyes.*

SIR ROWLAND *crosses and reluctantly exits to the library. The* INSPECTOR *closes the library door, then indicates to the Constable to sit* L *of the table up* C. CLARISSA *swings her feet off the sofa, and sits up. The* CONSTABLE *sits* L *of the table up* C, *and takes out his notebook and pencil*)

(*He moves to* L *of Clarissa*) Now, Mrs Hailsham-Brown, if you're ready. (*He picks up the cigarette box from the table* L *of the sofa, turns it over, opens it and looks at the cigarettes in it*)

CLARISSA. Dear Uncle Roly. He always wants to spare me everything. (*She sees the Inspector with the cigarette-box and becomes anxious. She smiles enchantingly at the Inspector*) This isn't going to be the third degree, is it?

INSPECTOR. Nothing of that kind. Just a few simple questions. (*To the Constable*) Are you ready, Jones? (*He pulls out the chair* R *of the bridge table, turns it and sits, facing Clarissa*)

CONSTABLE. All ready, sir.

INSPECTOR. Now, Mrs Hailsham-Brown, you had no idea that a body was concealed in that recess?

(*During the ensuing speeches, the* CONSTABLE *records the questions and answers*)

CLARISSA (*wide-eyed*) No, of course not. It's horrible—(*she shivers*) quite horrible.

INSPECTOR. When we were searching this room, why didn't you call our attention to that recess?

CLARISSA. D'you know, the thought never struck me. You see we never use it, so it never came into my head.

INSPECTOR. But you said you had just been through there into the library.

CLARISSA (*quickly*) Oh, no. You must have misunderstood me. (*She points to the library door*) What I meant was that door.

INSPECTOR (*rather grimly*) I certainly misunderstood you. Now you've no idea when Mr Costello came back to this house, or what he came for?

CLARISSA. I simply can't imagine.

INSPECTOR. But the fact remains that he did come back.

CLARISSA. Yes, of course.

INSPECTOR. He must have had some reason.

CLARISSA. I suppose so.

INSPECTOR. Perhaps he wanted to see your husband?

CLARISSA (*quickly*) Oh, no, I'm quite sure he didn't. Henry and he never liked each other.

INSPECTOR. Oh! Had there been a quarrel between them?

CLARISSA (*quickly*) Oh no, they haven't quarrelled. Henry just thought he wore the wrong shoes. (*She smiles*) You know how odd men are.

INSPECTOR. He didn't come back here to see you?

CLARISSA. Me? Oh no, I'm sure he didn't.

INSPECTOR. Is there anybody else in the house he might have wanted to see?

CLARISSA. I can't think who. I mean, who is there?

(*The* INSPECTOR *rises, turns his chair and puts it into the bridge table*)

INSPECTOR. Mr Costello comes here, returns the articles which the first Mrs Hailsham-Brown had taken away. He says "good-bye", then comes back here—(*he crosses to the french windows*) presumably through this window—he is killed—his body is pushed into that recess—(*he moves above the sofa*) all in a space of about ten—twenty minutes, and nobody hears anything.

CLARISSA. I know. (*She turns to the Inspector*) It's extraordinary, isn't it?

INSPECTOR. You're sure you didn't hear anything?

CLARISSA. Nothing. It really is fantastic.

INSPECTOR (*grimly*) Almost too fantastic. (*He pauses, then crosses to the hall door*) That's all for the present, Mrs Hailsham-Brown.

(CLARISSA *rises and goes rather quickly to the library door*)

(*He intercepts Clarissa*) Not that way. (*He opens the hall door*)

CLARISSA (*pausing by the library door*) I think, really, I'd rather join the others.

INSPECTOR. Later.

(CLARISSA *rather reluctantly crosses and exits to the hall*)

(*He closes the hall door, then moves to* L *of the Constable*) Where's the other woman? Miss—er—Peake?

CONSTABLE (*rising*) Put her on the spare room bed. After she came out of the hysterics, that is. Terrible time I had with her, laughing and crying something terrible she was.

INSPECTOR. Doesn't matter if Mrs H. B. goes and talks to her. But not to those three there. We'll have no comparing of stories, no prompting. You locked the door from the library to the hall?

CONSTABLE. Yes, sir. I've got the key here.

INSPECTOR. Good, we'll take them one at a time. (*He moves to* L *of the bridge table*) But first I'll have a word with that butler chap.

CONSTABLE. Elgin?

INSPECTOR. Yes, call him in. I've an idea he knows something.

CONSTABLE. Yes, indeed, sir. (*He moves to the hall door, opens it and calls*) Elgin, come you in here, please.

(*The* INSPECTOR *pulls out the chair* L *of the bridge table, then stands above the table.*

ELGIN, *when the door opens, is standing on the stairs, and starts to go guiltily up them. When the* CONSTABLE *calls,* ELGIN *stops, turns and comes into the room. The* CONSTABLE *closes the hall door and resumes his seat up* C)

INSPECTOR (*indicating the chair* L *of the table*) Sit down, Elgin.

(ELGIN *sits* L *of the bridge table*)

Now, you started off for the pictures this evening—(*he moves above the left end of the sofa*) but you came back. Why was that?

ELGIN. I've told you, sir, my wife wasn't feeling well.

INSPECTOR. It was you who let Mr Costello into the house when he called here this evening.

ELGIN. Yes, sir.

INSPECTOR (*moving to* R *of the bridge table*) Why didn't you tell us at once that it was Mr Costello's car outside?

ELGIN. I didn't know, sir. Mr Costello didn't drive up to the front door—I didn't know he'd come in a car.

INSPECTOR (*moving below the left end of the sofa*) Rather peculiar, eh?

ELGIN. Yes, sir. I expect he had his reasons.

INSPECTOR (*turning to Elgin*) Just what do you mean by that?

ELGIN (*smugly*) Nothing, sir. Nothing at all.

INSPECTOR (*sharply*) Ever seen Mr Costello before?

ELGIN. Never, sir.

INSPECTOR (*meaningly*) It wasn't because of Mr Costello that you came back this evening?

ELGIN. I've told you, sir, my wife . .

INSPECTOR. I don't want to hear any more about your wife. (*He moves down* R) How long have you been with Mrs Hailsham-Brown?

ELGIN. Six weeks, sir.

INSPECTOR (*turning to Elgin*) And before that?

ELGIN (*uneasily*) I'd—I'd been having a little rest.

INSPECTOR (*crossing to* R *of the bridge table*) A rest? You realize that in a case like this, your—(*he moves below the left end of the sofa*) references will have to be looked into very carefully.

ELGIN (*half rising*) Would that be . . .? (*He resumes his seat*) I —I wouldn't wish to deceive you, sir. It wasn't anything really wrong—what I mean is—the original reference having got torn— I couldn't quite remember the wording . . .

INSPECTOR (*moving to* R *of the bridge table; with ferocious geniality*) So you wrote your own references—that's what it comes to.

ELGIN. I didn't mean any harm. I've got my living to earn . . .

INSPECTOR (*interrupting*) At the moment, I'm not interested in fake references. I want to know what happened here tonight, and what you know about Mr Costello.

ELGIN. I'd never set eyes on him before. (*He looks round at the hall door*) But I've a good idea of why he came here.

INSPECTOR. Why?

ELGIN. Blackmail—he had something on *her*.

INSPECTOR (*moving up* R *of the bridge table*) On Mrs Hailsham-Brown?

ELGIN (*eagerly*) Yes. I came in to ask if there was anything more, and I heard them.

INSPECTOR. What did you hear exactly?

ELGIN (*dramatically*) I heard her say, "But that's blackmail. I'll not submit to it."

INSPECTOR (*a little doubtfully*) Hm! Anything more?

ELGIN. No—they stopped when *I* came in—and when I went out they dropped their voices.

INSPECTOR. I see.

ELGIN (*rising; whining*) You'll not be hard on me, sir. I've had a lot of trouble one way and another.

INSPECTOR. Get out.

ELGIN (*quickly*) Yes, sir. Thank you, sir.

(ELGIN *exits quickly to the hall*)

INSPECTOR (*moving to* R *of the Constable*) Blackmail—eh?

CONSTABLE (*primly*) And Mrs Hailsham-Brown such a nice seeming lady.

INSPECTOR (*curtly*) I'll see Mr Birch, now. (*He moves* C)

(*The* CONSTABLE *rises, turns to the library door and opens it*)

CONSTABLE (*calling*) Mr Birch, please.

(HUGO *enters from the library. He looks dogged and rather defiant. The* CONSTABLE *closes the library door and resumes his seat at the table up* C)

INSPECTOR (*pleasantly*) Come in, Mr Birch. (*He indicates the chair above the bridge table*) Sit down here, please.

(HUGO *sits above the bridge table*)

(*He crosses above Hugo to* L *of the bridge table*) A very unpleasant business, I'm afraid, sir. What have you to say about it? (*He tucks the chair* L *of the table underneath it*)

HUGO (*slapping his spectacle case on the table; defiantly*) Nothing.

INSPECTOR. Nothing?

HUGO. What do you expect me to say? The blinking woman snaps open the blinking cupboard and out falls a blinking corpse. Took my breath away. I've not got over it yet. It's no good asking me anything because I don't know anything.

INSPECTOR. That's your statement, is it? You know nothing at all about it?

HUGO. I'm telling you. I didn't kill the fellow. I didn't even know him.

INSPECTOR. You didn't know him. But you'd heard of him?

HUGO. Yes, and I heard he was a nasty bit of goods.

INSPECTOR. In what way?

HUGO. Oh, I don't know. Fellow that women liked and men had no use for. That sort of thing.

INSPECTOR. You've no idea why he should come back to this house a second time this evening?

HUGO. Not a clue.

INSPECTOR (*crossing above Hugo to* C) Anything between him and the present Mrs Hailsham-Brown, do you think?

HUGO (*shocked*) Clarissa? Good Lord, no! Nice girl, Clarissa. Got a lot of sense. Wouldn't look twice at a fellow like that.

INSPECTOR. So you can't help us?

HUGO. Sorry. There it is.

INSPECTOR (*moving above the sofa*) You'd no idea that the body was in that recess?

HUGO. Of course not.

INSPECTOR. Thank you, sir.

HUGO (*vaguely*) What?

INSPECTOR. That's all, thank you, sir. (*He moves to the desk and picks up the copy of* "Who's Who")

(HUGO *rises, picks up his spectacle case and moves to the library door, but the* CONSTABLE *rises and bars his way.* HUGO *turns towards the french windows*)

CONSTABLE (*moving to the hall door*) This way, Mr Birch, please.

(HUGO *exits to the hall. The* CONSTABLE *closes the door. The*
INSPECTOR *brings the book to the bridge table*)

He was a mine of information, wasn't he? (*He moves to* R *of the*
Inspector) Mind you, not very nice for a J.P. to be mixed up in a
murder.

(*The* INSPECTOR *sits above the bridge table and searches the book*)

INSPECTOR (*reading*) "Delahaye, Sir Rowland Edward Mark,
K.C.B., M.V.O. . . ."
CONSTABLE. What have you got there? (*He peers over the*
Inspector's shoulder) Who's Who.
INSPECTOR (*reading*) "Educated Eton—Trinity College . . ."
Um! "Attached Foreign Office—second Secretary—Madrid—
Plenipotentiary . . ."
CONSTABLE. Ooh!
INSPECTOR (*after a surprised look at the Constable*) " Constan-
tinople Foreign Office—special commission rendered—Clubs—
Boodles—Whites."
CONSTABLE. Do you want *him* next, sir?
INSPECTOR. No. I'll leave him till the last. We'll have young
Warrender.

(*The* CONSTABLE *moves to the library door and opens it*)

CONSTABLE (*calling*) Mr Warrender, please.

(JEREMY *enters from the library. He is attempting rather unsuc-*
cessfully to look quite at ease. The CONSTABLE *closes the library door*
and resumes his seat at the table up C. *The* INSPECTOR *half rises and*
pulls out the chair R *of the bridge table*)

INSPECTOR (*resuming his seat*) Sit down.

(JEREMY *sits* R *of the bridge table*)

Your name?
JEREMY. Jeremy Warrender.
INSPECTOR. Address?
JEREMY. Three hundred and forty Broad Street, and thirty-
four Grosvenor Square. Country address, Hepplestone, Wiltshire.
INSPECTOR. A gentleman of independent means?
JEREMY. No. I'm private secretary to Sir Lazarus Stein. Those
are his addresses.
INSPECTOR. How long have you been with him?
JEREMY. About a year.
INSPECTOR. Did you know this man Oliver Costello?
JEREMY. Never heard of him till tonight.
INSPECTOR. You didn't see him when he came to the house
earlier this evening?
JEREMY. No. I'd gone over to the golf club with the others. We

were dining there, you see. It was the servants' night out and Mr
Birch had asked us to dine with him at the club.

INSPECTOR. Was Mrs Hailsham-Brown asked, too?

JEREMY. No.

(*The* INSPECTOR *raises his eyebrows*)

(*He hurries on*) That is, she could have come if she'd liked.

INSPECTOR. She was asked, then? And she refused?

JEREMY (*getting rattled*) No. No. What I mean is—well, Hailsham-Brown is usually quite tired when he gets down here, and
Clarissa said they'd just have a scratch meal here, as usual.

INSPECTOR. So Mrs Hailsham-Brown expected her husband to
dine here? She didn't expect him to go out again as soon as he
came in?

JEREMY (*definitely flustered*) I—er—well—er—really I don't
know. No—I believe she did say he was going to be out this
evening.

INSPECTOR (*rising and crossing above Jeremy to* R *of him*) It seems
odd then that Mrs Hailsham-Brown should not come out to the
club, instead of remaining here to dine all by herself.

JEREMY (*turning on his chair to face the Inspector*) Well—er—well
—(*quickly*) I mean it was the kid—Pippa, you know. Clarissa
wouldn't have liked to go out to leave the kid all by herself in the
house.

INSPECTOR (*significantly*) Or perhaps she was making plans to
receive a visitor of her own?

JEREMY (*rising; hotly*) I say, that's a rotten thing to say. And
it isn't true. I'm sure she never planned anything of the kind.

INSPECTOR. Yet Oliver Costello came here to meet someone.
The servants were out. Miss Peake has her own cottage. There
was really no-one he could have come to the house to meet except
Mrs Hailsham-Brown.

JEREMY. All I can say is—(*he turns away*) you ask her.

INSPECTOR. I have asked her.

JEREMY. What did she say?

INSPECTOR (*easily*) Just what you say, Mr Warrender.

JEREMY (*sitting* R *of the bridge table*) There you are.

(*The* INSPECTOR *moves a step or two down* R *then turns and moves* C)

INSPECTOR. Now tell me how you all happened to come back
here from the club. Was that the original plan?

JEREMY. Yes. I mean, no.

INSPECTOR. Which do you mean, sir?

JEREMY. Well, it was like this. We all went over to the club.
Rowland and old Hugo went straight into the dining-room and
I came in a bit later. It's all a cold buffet, you know. I'd been
knocking balls about till it got dark and then, well, somebody

said "Bridge?" and I said, "Well, why not come back and play here?" So we did.

INSPECTOR. I see. It was your idea?

JEREMY. I don't remember who suggested it first. Hugo Birch, I think.

INSPECTOR. And you arrived back here—when?

JEREMY. Can't say exactly. Probably left the club house just a bit before eight.

INSPECTOR. And it's what—five minutes' walk?

JEREMY. Just about. The golf course adjoin this garden.

INSPECTOR (*crossing below the bridge table to* L) And then you played bridge?

JEREMY. Yes.

INSPECTOR (*moving to* L *of the table*) That must have been about twenty minutes before my arrival. (*He moves above the table*) Surely you hadn't time to complete two rubbers and start—(*he shows Jeremy Clarissa's marker*) a third?

JEREMY. What? Oh, no. No. That first rubber must have been yesterday's score.

INSPECTOR (*indicating the other markers*) Only one person seems to have scored.

JEREMY. Yes. I'm afraid we're all a bit lazy about scoring. We left it to Clarissa.

INSPECTOR (*crossing to* L *of the sofa*) Did you know about the passage-way between this room and the library?

JEREMY. You mean the place the body was found?

INSPECTOR. That's what I mean.

JEREMY. No. No, I'd no idea. Wonderful bit of camouflage, isn't it? You'd never guess.

(*The* INSPECTOR *sits on the left arm of the sofa, slips back a little, dislodges the cushion and sees the gloves*)

INSPECTOR. Consequently you couldn't know there was a body in it. Could you?

JEREMY (*turning away*) You could have knocked me over with a feather, as the saying goes.

(*The* INSPECTOR *sorts out the gloves*)

Absolute blood and thunder melodrama. Couldn't believe my eyes.

(*The* INSPECTOR *holds up one of the pairs of gloves, rather in the manner of a conjuror*)

INSPECTOR. Are these your gloves, Mr Warrender?

JEREMY (*turning to the Inspector*) No. I mean, yes.

INSPECTOR. You were wearing them when you came over from the golf club?

JEREMY. Yes. There's a bit of a nip in the air this evening.

INSPECTOR (*rising and moving to* R *of Jeremy*) I think you're mistaken. (*He indicates the initials in the gloves*) These have Mr Hailsham-Brown's initials inside them.

JEREMY. Oh, funny. I've got a pair just the same.

(*The* INSPECTOR *returns to the sofa, sits on the left arm and produces the second pair of gloves*)

INSPECTOR. These perhaps?

JEREMY. You don't catch me a second time. (*He laughs*) After all, one pair of gloves looks exactly like another.

INSPECTOR (*producing the third pair of gloves*) Three pairs of gloves. (*He examines the gloves*) All with Hailsham-Brown's initials inside. Curious.

JEREMY. Well, it is his house, after all. Why shouldn't he have three pairs of gloves lying about?

INSPECTOR. The only interesting thing is that you thought one of them might have been yours. And I think that your gloves are just sticking out of your pocket, now.

(JEREMY *puts his hand in his right-hand pocket*)

No, the other pocket.

JEREMY (*taking his gloves from his left-hand pocket*) Oh, yes. Yes, so they are.

INSPECTOR. They're not really very like these. Are they?

JEREMY. Actually, these are my golfing gloves.

INSPECTOR. Thank you, Mr Warrender. (*He puts back the cushion*) That's all for now.

JEREMY (*rises; upset*) Look here, you don't think . . .

INSPECTOR. I don't think what?

JEREMY. Nothing. (*He rises and moves to the library door*)

(*The* CONSTABLE *rises and intercepts* JEREMY, *who turns to the Inspector and points to the hall door. The* INSPECTOR *nods.*

JEREMY *exits to the hall, closing the door. The* INSPECTOR *leaves the gloves on the sofa, moves to the bridge table, sits above it and looks through* "*Who's Who*")

INSPECTOR. Here we are. (*He reads*) "Stein, Sir Lazarus. Chairman of Saxon-Arabian Oil Company, Gulf Petroleum Company. Clubs . . ." Hmm! "Recreations: Philately, golf, fishing. Address, three hundred and forty Broad Street, thirty-four Grosvenor Square."

(*The* CONSTABLE, *while the Inspector is reading, moves to the table* L *of the sofa and sharpens his pencil into the ashtray. He stoops to pick up some shavings from the floor, finds the playing card left by Pippa, brings it to the bridge table and throws it down*)

What have you got there?

CONSTABLE. Just a card, sir. Found it over there, under the sofa.

INSPECTOR (*picking up the card*) The Ace of Spades. A very interesting card. Here, wait a minute. (*He turns the card over*) Red. Same pack. (*He picks up the red pack of cards from the table and spreads them out*)

(*The* CONSTABLE *helps the Inspector to sort through the cards*)

Well, well, no Ace of Spades. (*He rises*) Now, that's very remarkable, don't you think, Jones? (*He puts the card in his pocket and crosses to* L *of the sofa*)

CONSTABLE (*tidying the cards on the table*) Very remarkable indeed, sir.

INSPECTOR (*collecting the gloves from the sofa*) Now, we'll have Sir Rowland Delahaye. (*He brings the gloves to the bridge table and puts them in pairs on the table, in front of the upstage chair*)

(*The* CONSTABLE *goes to the library door and opens it*)

CONSTABLE (*calling*) Sir Rowland Delahaye.

(SIR ROWLAND *enters from the library*)

INSPECTOR. Come in, Sir Rowland. (*He indicates the chair above the bridge table*) Sit down, please.

(SIR ROWLAND *moves to the bridge table, sees the gloves, pauses a moment, then sits above the table*)

You are Sir Rowland Delahaye. (*He leans on the chair* R *of the table*) Your address?

SIR ROWLAND. Long Paddock, Littlewich Green, Lincolnshire. (*He touches the copy of* "Who's Who") Couldn't you find it, Inspector?

INSPECTOR. Now, if you please, I'd like *your* account of the evening, after you left here shortly before seven.

SIR ROWLAND. It had been raining all day, and it suddenly cleared up. We had already arranged to go to the golf club for dinner as it is the servants' night out. So we did that. As we were finishing dinner, Mrs Hailsham-Brown rang up and suggested that, as her husband had had unexpectedly to go out, we three should return here and make up a four for bridge. We did so. About twenty minutes after we'd started playing you arrived, Inspector. The rest—you know.

INSPECTOR. That's not quite Mr Warrender's account of the matter.

SIR ROWLAND. Indeed. How did he put it?

INSPECTOR. He said that the suggestion to come back here and play bridge came from one of you three. Mr Birch, he thought.

SIR ROWLAND (*easily*) Ah, but you see Warrender came into

the dining-room rather late. He did not realize that Mrs Hailsham-Brown had rung up.

(SIR ROWLAND *and the* INSPECTOR *measure glances. The* INSPECTOR *crosses above the bridge table to* L *of it*)

You must know better than I do, Inspector, how very rarely two people's account of the same thing agrees. In fact, if three people were to agree exactly, I should regard it as suspicious. Very suspicious, indeed.

INSPECTOR (*sitting* L *of the table*) I'd like to discuss the case with you, sir, if I may?

SIR ROWLAND. How very agreeable of you, Inspector.

INSPECTOR. The dead man, Mr Oliver Costello, came to this house with some particular object in view. Do you agree to that, sir?

SIR ROWLAND. He came to return certain objects which Mrs Miranda Hailsham-Brown had taken away in error.

INSPECTOR. That may have been his excuse, sir, though I'm not even sure of that. But it wasn't the real reason that brought him here.

SIR ROWLAND. You may be right. I can't say.

INSPECTOR. He came, perhaps, to see a particular person. It may have been you, it may have been Mr Warrender, it may have been Mr Birch.

SIR ROWLAND. If he had wanted to see Mr Birch he would have gone to his house, he wouldn't have come here.

INSPECTOR. That is probably so. Therefore, that leaves us with the choice of four people. You, Mr Warrender, Mr Hailsham-Brown and Mrs Hailsham-Brown. Now how well did you know Oliver Costello?

SIR ROWLAND. Hardly at all. I've met him once or twice, that's all.

INSPECTOR. Where did you meet him?

SIR ROWLAND (*reflecting*) Twice at the Hailsham-Browns' in London, over a year ago, and once in a restaurant, I believe.

INSPECTOR. But you had no reason for wishing to murder him?

SIR ROWLAND (*smiling*) Is that an accusation, Inspector?

INSPECTOR. No, Sir Rowland. I should call it more an elimination. I don't think you have any motive for doing away with Oliver Costello. That leaves three people.

SIR ROWLAND. This sounds like a variant of Ten Little Nigger Boys.

(*The* INSPECTOR *smiles, rises and crosses below the table to* R *of Sir Rowland*)

INSPECTOR. We'll take Mr Warrender. How well do you know him?

SIR ROWLAND. I met him here for the first time two days ago.

He appears to be an agreeable young man, well bred, well educated. I know nothing about him, but I should say an unlikely murderer.

INSPECTOR. So much for Mr Warrender. That brings me to my next question.

SIR ROWLAND (*anticipating*) How well do I know Henry Hailsham-Brown and how well do I know Mrs Hailsham-Brown. I know Henry Hailsham-Brown very well indeed. He is an old friend. Of Clarissa I know all there is to know. She is my ward and inexpressibly dear to me.

INSPECTOR. Yes, sir. I think that answer makes certain things very clear.

SIR ROWLAND. Does it, indeed?

INSPECTOR (*moving below the right end of the sofa*) Why did you change your plans this evening? Why did you come back here and pretend to play bridge?

SIR ROWLAND (*sharply*) Pretend?

INSPECTOR (*taking the playing card from his pocket and moving to R of Sir Rowland*) This card was found on the other side of the room under the sofa. I can hardly believe that you would have played two rubbers of bridge and started a third with a pack of fifty-one cards, and the Ace of Spades missing.

(SIR ROWLAND *takes the card from the Inspector, looks at the back of it and then returns it*)

SIR ROWLAND. Yes. Perhaps that is a little difficult to believe.

(*The* INSPECTOR *looks despairingly upwards*)

INSPECTOR. I also think that three pairs of Mr Hailsham-Brown's gloves need a certain amount of explanation.

SIR ROWLAND (*after a moment's pause*) I'm afraid, Inspector, you won't get any explanation from me.

INSPECTOR. No, sir. I take it that you are out to do your best for a certain lady. But it's not a bit of good, sir. Truth will out.

SIR ROWLAND. I wonder.

INSPECTOR (*moving to the panel*) Mrs Hailsham-Brown knew that body was in the recess. Whether she dragged it there herself, or whether you helped her, I don't know. But she knew. (*He moves to R of Sir Rowland*) Now, I suggest that Oliver Costello came here to see Mrs Hailsham-Brown and to obtain money from her by threats.

SIR ROWLAND. Threats? Threats of what?

INSPECTOR. That will come out, no doubt. Mrs Hailsham-Brown is young and attractive, gay. This Mr Costello was attractive to the ladies, they say. Now Mrs Hailsham-Brown is newly married and . . .

SIR ROWLAND. Stop! I must put you right on certain matters. You can confirm what I tell you easily enough. Henry Hailsham-

Brown's first marriage was unfortunate. His wife was a beautiful woman, but unbalanced and neurotic. Her health and disposition had degenerated to such an alarming state that her little daughter had to be removed to a nursing home. Yes, a really shocking state of affairs. It seemed that she had become a drug addict. How she obtained these drugs was not found out, but it was a very fair guess that she had been supplied with them by this man, Oliver Costello. She was infatuated with him and finally ran away with him. Henry Hailsham-Brown allowed her to divorce him. He's old-fashioned in his views. He has now found happiness and peace in his marriage with Clarissa and I can assure you, Inspector, that there are no guilty secrets in Clarissa's life. There is nothing, I can swear, with which Costello could possibly threaten her. (*He rises, tucks his chair under the table, moves L. of it, then crosses and stands below the right end of the sofa*) Don't you think, Inspector, that you're on the wrong tack altogether? Why should you be so certain it was a person Costello came here to see? Why couldn't it have been a place?

INSPECTOR. What do you mean, sir?

SIR ROWLAND (*moving above the right end of the sofa*) When you were talking to us about the late Mr Sellon, you mentioned that the Narcotic Squad took an interest in him. Isn't there a possible link there? Drugs—Sellon—Sellon's house—(*he moves above the left end of the sofa*) Costello has been here once before, I understand, ostensibly to look at Sellon's antiques. Supposing Oliver Costello wanted something in this house. In that desk perhaps.

(*The* INSPECTOR *looks at the desk*)

There is the curious incident of a man who came here and offered an exorbitant price for that desk. Supposing it was that desk that Oliver Costello wanted to examine—search, if you like. Supposing that he was followed here by someone. And that that someone struck him down, there by the desk.

INSPECTOR. There's a good deal of supposition . . .

SIR ROWLAND. It's a very reasonable hypothesis, I think.

INSPECTOR. The hypothesis being that this somebody put the body in the recess?

SIR ROWLAND. Exactly.

INSPECTOR. That would mean someone who knew about the recess.

SIR ROWLAND. Someone who knew the house in the *Sellons'* time.

INSPECTOR (*rather impatiently*) Yes—that's all very well, sir, but it still doesn't explain one thing . . .

SIR ROWLAND. What's that?

INSPECTOR. Mrs Hailsham-Brown knew the body was in that recess. She tried to prevent us looking there. It's no good trying to convince me otherwise. She knew. (*He moves L*)

SIR ROWLAND (*after a pause*) Inspector. Will you allow me to speak to my ward?

INSPECTOR. Only in my presence, sir.

SIR ROWLAND. That will do.

INSPECTOR (*moving to* L *of Sir Rowland*) Jones!

(*The* CONSTABLE *rises and exits to the hall*)

SIR ROWLAND. We are very much in your hands, Inspector. I will ask you to make what allowances you can.

(*The* CONSTABLE *enters from the hall and holds the door open*)

CONSTABLE. Come in here, please, Mrs Hailsham-Brown.

(CLARISSA *enters from the hall.* SIR ROWLAND *crosses to her, and speaks very solemnly. The* INSPECTOR *moves to* R *of the sofa*)

SIR ROWLAND. Clarissa, my dear. Will you do what I ask you? Tell the Inspector the truth.

CLARISSA (*doubtfully*) The truth?

SIR ROWLAND (*with emphasis*) The truth. It's the only thing to do.

(SIR ROWLAND *looks at Clarissa for a moment, then exits to the hall. The* CONSTABLE *closes the door, then resumes his seat up* C)

INSPECTOR (*indicating the sofa*) Sit down, Mrs Hailsham-Brown.

(CLARISSA *smiles at the* INSPECTOR, *but he looks stern. She moves slowly to the sofa, sits and waits a moment before she speaks*)

CLARISSA. I'm sorry. I'm terribly sorry I told you all those lies. I didn't mean to. (*Ruefully*) One gets into things, if you know what I mean?

INSPECTOR (*coldly*) I can't say that I do know. Now, give me the facts, please.

CLARISSA. Well, it's really all quite simple. (*She ticks these off*) Oliver left; then Henry came home; then I saw him off again in the car; then I came in here with the sandwiches.

INSPECTOR. Sandwiches?

CLARISSA. Yes. You see my husband is bringing home a very important delegate from abroad.

INSPECTOR. Oh, who is this delegate?

CLARISSA. A Mr Jones.

INSPECTOR (*with a look at the Constable*) I beg your pardon.

CLARISSA. They were going to have the sandwiches while they talked and I was going to have mousse in the schoolroom.

INSPECTOR. Mousse in the . . . Yes, I see . . .

CLARISSA. I put the sandwiches down there—(*she points to the stool*) then I began tidying up and I went to put a book back in the bookshelf and—then—and then I practically fell over it.

INSPECTOR. You fell over the body?

CLARISSA. Yes. It was here behind the sofa. And I looked to see if it—if he was dead, and he was. It was Oliver Costello and I didn't know what to do. In the end I rang up the golf club and I asked Sir Rowland, Mr Birch and Jeremy Warrender to come over.

INSPECTOR (*leaning over the right end of the sofa; coldly*) It didn't occur to you to ring up the police?

CLARISSA. It occurred to me, yes, but then—well—(*she smiles*) I didn't.

INSPECTOR. You didn't. (*He crosses behind the sofa, looks at the Constable, lifts his hands despairingly, then moves to L of the sofa*) Why not?

CLARISSA. Well, I didn't think it would be nice for my husband. I don't know whether you know many people in the Foreign Office, Inspector, but they're frightfully unassuming. They like everything very quiet, not noticeable. You must admit that murders are noticeable.

INSPECTOR. Quite so.

CLARISSA (*warmly*) I'm so glad you understand. (*Her story becomes more and more unconvincing as she feels that she is not making headway*) I mean, he was quite dead because I felt his pulse, so we couldn't do anything for him.

(*The* INSPECTOR *moves a step down* L)

What I mean is, he might be just as well dead in Marsden Wood as in our drawing-room.

INSPECTOR (*turning sharply to her*) Marsden Wood? Where's Marsden Wood come into it?

CLARISSA. That's where I was thinking of putting him.

(*The* INSPECTOR *puts a hand to the back of his head, moves up* L, *then crosses to* L *of Clarissa*)

INSPECTOR (*firmly*) Mrs Hailsham-Brown, have you never heard that a dead body, if there's any suggestion of foul play, should never be moved?

CLARISSA. Of course I know that, it says so in all the detective stories, but you see this is real life.

(*The* INSPECTOR *lifts his hands in despair*)

I mean, real life's quite different.

INSPECTOR. Do you realize the seriousness of what you're saying?

CLARISSA. Of course I do, and I'm telling you the truth. So, you see, in the end I rang up the club and they all came over.

INSPECTOR. And you persuaded them to hide the body in that recess.

CLARISSA. No. That came later. My plan, as I told you, was

that they should take Oliver's body away in his car and leave the car in Marsden Wood.

INSPECTOR (*unbelievingly*) And they agreed?

CLARISSA. They agreed. (*She smiles at him*)

INSPECTOR (*moving down* L; *brusquely*) Frankly, Mrs Hailsham-Brown, I don't believe a word of it. (*He turns and moves to* L *of Clarissa*) I don't believe that three reputable men would agree to obstruct the course of justice in such a manner for such a paltry cause.

CLARISSA (*rising and moving down* R; *to herself more than to the Inspector*) I knew you wouldn't believe me if I told you the truth. (*She turns to him*) What do you believe then?

INSPECTOR (*crossing between the sofa and stool to* L *of Clarissa; watching her*) I can see only one reason why those three men should agree to lie.

CLARISSA. Oh, you mean . . .? (*She pauses*)

INSPECTOR. If they believed—or *knew*—that *you* had killed him.

CLARISSA. But I had no reason for killing him. Absolutely no reason. (*She crosses below the stool and stands below the bridge table*) Oh, I knew you'd react like this. That's why . . . (*She breaks off*)

INSPECTOR (*turning to her*) That's why what?

(CLARISSA *thinks. Some moments pass, then her manner changes. From now on she is convincing*)

CLARISSA (*with the air of one making a clean breast of things*) All right, then. I'll tell you.

INSPECTOR (*moving to* L *of the stool*) I think it would be wiser.

CLARISSA (*turning to the Inspector*) Yes, I suppose I'd better tell you the *truth*.

INSPECTOR (*smiling*) I can assure you that telling the police a pack of lies will do you very little good, Mrs Hailsham-Brown. You'd better tell me the real story.

CLARISSA (*with a sigh*) I will. (*She sits in the chair* R *of the bridge table*) Oh dear, I thought I was being so clever.

INSPECTOR. Much better not to try to be clever. (*He sits on the left end of the stool, facing Clarissa*) Now then, what really did happen this evening?

CLARISSA. It all started as I explained. I said good-bye to Oliver and he'd gone off with Miss Peake. I had no idea he would come back again and I still can't understand why he did. Then, my husband came home, explaining he would have to go out again immediately. He went off in the car and it was just after I shut the front door, and made sure it was latched and bolted, that I suddenly began to feel nervous.

INSPECTOR. Nervous? Why?

CLARISSA (*acting her part with great feeling*) I'm not usually nervous, but it occurred to me that I'd never been alone in the house at night.

INSPECTOR. Well?

CLARISSA. Well, I told myself not to be so silly. I said to myself, "You've got the phone, haven't you? You can always ring for help." I said to myself, "Burglars don't come at this time of the evening. They come in the middle of the night." But I still kept thinking I heard a door shutting somewhere, footsteps up in my bedroom—so I thought I'd better do something.

INSPECTOR. Yes?

CLARISSA. I went into the kitchen and made the sandwiches for Henry and Mr Jones to have when they got back. I got them all ready on a plate with a napkin round them to keep them soft, and I was just coming across the hall to put them in here when— (*dramatically*) I *really* heard something.

INSPECTOR. Where?

CLARISSA. In this room. I knew that this time I wasn't imagining it. I heard drawers being pulled open and shut, then I suddenly remembered the window in here wasn't locked. Somebody had come in that way.

INSPECTOR. Go on, Mrs Hailsham-Brown.

CLARISSA. I didn't know what to do. I was petrified. Then I thought, "Suppose I'm just being a fool? Suppose it is Henry come back for something—or even Sir Rowland or one of the others. A nice fool you'll look if you go upstairs and ring the police on the extension." So then I thought of a plan.

INSPECTOR. Yes?

CLARISSA. I went to the hall stand and I took the heaviest stick I could find. I went into the library; I didn't turn the light on. I felt my way across the room to that recess. I opened it very gently and slipped inside. I thought I could ease the door into here and see who it was. (*She points to the panel*) Unless anyone knew about it you'd never dream there was a door just there.

INSPECTOR. No, you certainly wouldn't.

CLARISSA. I eased the catch open, then my fingers slipped, the door swung right open and hit against a chair. A man who was standing by the desk straightened up. I saw something bright and shining in his hand. I thought it was a revolver. I was terrified. I thought he was going to shoot me. I hit out at him with the stick with all my might and he fell. (*She collapses and leans on the table with her face in her hands*) Could I—could I have a little brandy, please?

INSPECTOR (*rising and moving up* C) Yes, of course. Jones!

(*The* CONSTABLE *rises, pours some brandy into a glass and hands it to the Inspector.* CLARISSA *lifts her face but covers it again and holds out her hand as the* INSPECTOR *brings her the drink.* CLARISSA *drinks, coughs, returns the glass to the* INSPECTOR, *who hands it to the* CONSTABLE, *who replaces the glass on the table up* C *and resumes his seat*)

(*He stands* R *of Clarissa*) Do you feel able to continue, Mrs Hailsham-Brown?

CLARISSA. Yes. You're very kind. (*She turns to the Inspector*) The man just lay there. He didn't move. I switched on the light and I saw then that it was Oliver Costello. He was dead. It was terrible. I—I couldn't understand it—(*she gestures towards the desk*) what was he doing there, tampering with the desk? It was all like some ghastly nightmare. I was so frightened I rang the golf club. I wanted my guardian. They all came over. I begged them to help me, to take the body away—somewhere.

INSPECTOR. But why?

CLARISSA (*turning away*) Because I was a coward. A miserable coward. I was frightened of the publicity, of having to go to a police court. And it would be so bad for my husband and for his career. (*She turns to the Inspector*) If it had really been a burglar perhaps I could have gone through with it, but being someone we actually knew, someone who is married to Henry's first wife . . . Oh, I just felt I couldn't go through with it.

INSPECTOR. Possibly because the dead man had, a short while before, attempted to blackmail you?

CLARISSA (*with complete confidence*) Blackmail me? Oh, nonsense! That's just silly. There's nothing anyone could blackmail me about.

INSPECTOR. Elgin, the butler, overheard a mention of blackmail.

CLARISSA. I don't believe he heard anything of the kind. He couldn't. If you ask me he's making the whole thing up. (*She pauses and blinks*)

INSPECTOR. Come now, Mrs Hailsham-Brown, do you deliberately tell me that the word blackmail was never mentioned?

CLARISSA (*banging the table with her left hand*) I swear it wasn't. I assure you . . . (*Her hand stops in mid-air and she laughs*) Oh, how silly. Of course. That was it.

INSPECTOR. You've remembered?

CLARISSA. It was nothing really. It was just that Oliver was saying something about the rent of furnished houses being absurdly high and I said we'd been amazingly lucky and were only paying four guineas a week for this. And he said, "I can hardly believe it, Clarissa. What's your pull? It must be blackmail." And I laughed and said, "That's it. Blackmail." (*She laughs*) Just a silly, joking way of talking. Why, I didn't even remember it.

INSPECTOR. I'm sorry, Mrs Hailsham-Brown, but I really can't believe that.

CLARISSA. Can't believe what?

INSPECTOR. That you're only paying four guineas a week furnished here.

CLARISSA (*rising*) You really are the most unbelieving man

I've ever met. You don't seem to believe a single thing I've said to you this evening. Most things I can't prove, but this one I can. And this time I'm going to show you. (*She crosses to the desk, opens a drawer and searches through the papers in it*)

(*The* INSPECTOR *moves up* C)

Here it is. No, it isn't. Ah! Here we are. (*She takes a document from the drawer, moves to* R *of the Inspector and shows it to him*) Here's the agreement for a furnished tenancy. It's with a firm of solicitors acting for the executors and, see, *four guineas per week.*

INSPECTOR (*jolted*) Well, I'm blessed! It's extraordinary. Quite extraordinary.

CLARISSA (*with charm*) Don't you think, Inspector, that you ought to beg my pardon?

INSPECTOR (*responding*) I apologize, Mrs Hailsham-Brown, but it really is extremely odd.

CLARISSA. Why?

INSPECTOR (*moving down* C) It so happens——

(CLARISSA *moves to the desk and replaces the document in the drawer*)

——a lady and gentleman were down here with orders to view this house——

(CLARISSA *moves to* L *of the sofa*)

——and the lady happened to lose a very valuable brooch. She called in at the police station to give particulars and she happened to mention this house. She said they were asking an absurd price. She thought eighteen guineas a week for a house right in the country and miles from anywhere was ridiculous. I agreed with her.

CLARISSA. Yes, that is extraordinary, very extraordinary. (*She smiles*) I understand why you were sceptical. But perhaps now you'll believe some of the other things I said.

INSPECTOR. I'm not doubting your *final* story, Mrs Hailsham-Brown. We usually know the truth when we hear it. I knew too, that there would have to be some serious reason for those three gentlemen to cook up this harebrained scheme of concealment.

CLARISSA (*with a step towards him*) You mustn't blame them too much, Inspector. It was my fault. I went on and on at them.

INSPECTOR (*conscious of her charm*) Ah, I've no doubt you did. But what I don't understand is, who telephoned the police?

CLARISSA (*startled*) How extraordinary! Yes, I'd forgotten *that.*

INSPECTOR. It clearly wasn't you, and it wouldn't be any of the three gentlemen . . .

CLARISSA (*to herself*) Elgin, Miss Peake . . .

INSPECTOR. Not Miss Peake. She didn't know the body was there.

Clarissa (*thoughtfully*) I wonder . . .

Inspector. Why, when the body was discovered she had hysterics.

Clarissa. Oh, anyone can have hysterics.

(Clarissa *realizes what she has said. The* Inspector *does a double-take.* Clarissa *smiles at him*)

Inspector. Anyway, she doesn't live in the house. She has her own cottage.

Clarissa. She could have been in the house. She has keys to all the doors.

Inspector (*moving a step to* l) It looks to me more like Elgin who telephoned.

Clarissa (*moving to* r *of the Inspector*) You won't send me to prison, will you? Uncle Roly said you wouldn't.

Inspector (*austerely*) It's a good thing you changed your story in time and told the truth, madam. If you'll let me advise you, Mrs Hailsham-Brown, you'll get in touch with your solicitor as soon as possible. In the meantime, I'll get your statement typed out and read over to you and perhaps you will sign it.

(Sir Rowland *enters from the hall*)

Sir Rowland. I couldn't keep away any longer. (*He moves up* l *of the bridge table*) Inspector, is it all right? Do you understand?

Clarissa (*crossing below the Inspector to* r *of Sir Rowland*) Roly, darling. (*She holds his hand*) I've made a statement and the police —(*she turns to the Inspector*) Mr Jones—is going to type it. Then I've got to sign it and I've told them everything.

(*The* Inspector *moves to the Constable*)

(*With emphasis*) How I thought it was a burglar and hit him on the head——

(Sir Rowland *looks in alarm at Clarissa*)

—(*she covers Sir Rowland's mouth with her hand so that he cannot speak*) and then it turned out to be Oliver so I got in a terrible flap and rang you; and how I begged and begged and at last you gave in. I see now how wrong of me it was——

(*The* Inspector *moves* c, *level with Clarissa*)

—but at the time—(*she takes her hand from Sir Rowland's mouth*) I was just scared stiff and I thought it would be cosier for everybody, me, Henry, and even Miranda, if Oliver was found in Marsden Wood.

Sir Rowland (*completely taken aback*) Clarissa! What have you been saying?

Inspector (*complacently*) Mrs Hailsham-Brown has made a very full statement, sir.

SIR ROWLAND (*dryly*) So it seems.

CLARISSA. It was the best thing to do. It was the only thing to do. The Inspector made me see that.

INSPECTOR. It will lead to far less trouble in the end. Now, Mrs Hailsham-Brown, I shan't ask you to go into the recess while the body is there, but I'd like you to show me exactly where the man was standing when you came through that way.

CLARISSA. Oh—yes—well—he was . . . (*She crosses below the Inspector to the desk*) No—he was standing here like this. (*She stands at the upstage end of the desk*)

(*The* INSPECTOR *moves up* RC *and motions to the* CONSTABLE, *who rises and puts his hand on the panel switch*)

INSPECTOR. I see—Jones—and then the door opened.

(*The* CONSTABLE *actuates the switch and the panel opens.* CLARISSA *and the* INSPECTOR *move a little downstage. The recess is empty except for a small piece of paper*)

And you came through that way. (*He looks at the recess*) And then— (*he does a double-take*) what the hell! Where's the body?

(*The* CONSTABLE *goes into the recess and picks up the piece of paper. The* INSPECTOR *looks accusingly at Clarissa and Sir Rowland*)

CONSTABLE (*reading the paper*) "Sucks to you!"

The INSPECTOR *snatches the paper from the Constable and the front door bell peals loudly off as—*

the CURTAIN *falls*

ACT III

SCENE—*The same. A few minutes later.*

When the CURTAIN *rises the panel is closed.* SIR ROWLAND *is standing by the open hall doors looking into the hall.* CLARISSA *is standing* R *of Sir Rowland. Voices are heard off.*

INSPECTOR (*off*) I'm really very sorry, Doctor, but we did have a body.

DOCTOR (*off*) Really, Inspector Lord, to bring me all this way on a wild-goose chase.

INSPECTOR (*off*) But I assure you, Doctor, we did have a body.

HUGO (*off*) I can't think how you policemen ever get anything done: losing bodies.

CONSTABLE (*off*) The Inspector's right, Doctor, we did have a body.

JEREMY (*off*) I don't understand why a guard wasn't put on the body.

DOCTOR (*off*) Well, I'm not wasting any more time—you'll hear more about this, Inspector Lord.

INSPECTOR (*off*) Yes, Doctor. Good night, Doctor.

(*The front door slams off*)

Now, Elgin.

ELGIN (*off*) I know nothing about it, I assure you, sir, nothing at all.

(CLARISSA *giggles, moves and sits on the left arm of the sofa.* SIR ROWLAND *closes the hall doors and the voices fade*)

SIR ROWLAND (*moving* C) Rather a bad moment for the police reinforcement to arrive. The Divisional Surgeon, in particular, seems very annoyed at finding no corpse to examine.

CLARISSA (*giggling*) But who can have spirited it away? Do you think Jeremy managed it somehow?

SIR ROWLAND. I don't see how he could have done. They didn't let anyone back into the library and the door from the library to the hall was locked. Pippa's "Sucks to you" was the last straw.

(CLARISSA *laughs*)

Still it shows us one thing. Costello had opened the secret drawer. (*His manner changes*) Clarissa, why didn't you tell the truth to the Inspector?

CLARISSA. I did, except for the part about Pippa. (*She rises and sits* C *of the sofa*) He didn't believe me.

67

SIR ROWLAND. Why on earth did you have to stuff him with all that nonsense?

CLARISSA. It seemed to me the most likely thing the Inspector would believe. (*Triumphantly*) And he *has* believed me.

SIR ROWLAND. And a nice mess you're in now. Manslaughter for all you know.

CLARISSA. Self-defence.

(JEREMY *and* HUGO *enter from the hall, each opening one of the double doors.* SIR ROWLAND *moves above the left end of the sofa*)

HUGO (*moving to* L *of the bridge table; grumbling*) Pushing us around here and there. Now it seems they've gone and lost the body.

(JEREMY *closes the doors, crosses below the card table to the stool and takes a sandwich*)

JEREMY. Damn funny, I call it.

CLARISSA. It's fantastic. The whole thing's fantastic. Who rang up the police and said there'd been a murder here?

JEREMY (*sitting on the right arm of the sofa*) Elgin.

HUGO. That Peake woman.

CLARISSA. But *why*? It doesn't make sense.

(MISS PEAKE *enters from the hall, looking around her with a conspiratorial glance*)

MISS PEAKE. Hullo, coast clear? (*She closes the door and crosses to* C) No bobbies about? They seem to be swarming all over the place.

SIR ROWLAND. They're searching the house and grounds.

MISS PEAKE. What for?

SIR ROWLAND. The body. It's gone.

MISS PEAKE (*laughing*) What a lark! The disappearing body, eh?

HUGO (*sitting* L *of the bridge table; to the universe*) It's a nightmare. The whole thing's a damn nightmare.

MISS PEAKE. Quite like the films, eh, Mrs Brown-Hailsham?

SIR ROWLAND (*courteously*) I hope you are feeling better now, Miss Peake?

MISS PEAKE. Oh, I'm all right. Pretty tough really, you know. Just bowled over by opening that door and finding a corpse. Turned me up for the moment, I must admit.

CLARISSA. I wondered, perhaps, if you knew it was there?

MISS PEAKE (*staring at Clarissa*) Who? Me?

CLARISSA. Yes. You.

HUGO (*to the universe*) It doesn't make sense. Why take the body away? We all know there is a body, we know his identity and everything. No point in it.

MISS PEAKE (*leaning across the bridge table to Hugo*) Oh, I wouldn't say *that*, Mr Birch. You've got to *have* a body, you know. *Habeas Corpus* and all that. Remember? You've got to have a body before you can bring a charge of murder against anybody. (*She moves* c) So don't you worry, Mrs Brown-Hailsham. (*Reassuringly*) Everything's going to be all right.

CLARISSA. Me? Do you mean . . .?

MISS PEAKE. I've kept my ears open this evening. I haven't spent all my time lying on the spare room bed. I never liked that man Elgin, or his wife. Listening at doors, and running to the police with stories about blackmail.

CLARISSA. So you heard?

MISS PEAKE. What I always say is, stand by your own sex. (*She looks at Hugo*) Men! (*She snorts*) I don't hold with them. (*She sits* L *of Clarissa on the sofa*) If they can't find the body, my dear, they can't bring a charge against you. And I say, if that brute was blackmailing you, you did quite right to crack him over the head and good riddance.

(SIR ROWLAND *moves down* c)

CLARISSA (*faintly*) But I didn't . . .

MISS PEAKE. I heard you tell that Inspector all about it. And if it wasn't for that eavesdropping, skulking fellow Elgin, your story would sound quite all right.

CLARISSA. Which one?

MISS PEAKE. About mistaking him for a burglar. It's the black-mail angle that puts a different complexion on it all. So I thought there was only one thing to do; get rid of the body and let the police chase their tails looking for it.

(SIR ROWLAND *staggers down* c)

(*She looks complacently around*) Pretty smart work, if I say so myself.

JEREMY (*rising; fascinated*) D'you mean to say——

(*The others all stare at Miss Peake*)

—that it was you?

MISS PEAKE. We're all friends here, aren't we? (*She looks around*) Yes. I moved the body. (*She taps her pocket*) Locking the door! I've got keys to all the doors in this house.

CLARISSA. But how? Where—where did you put it?

MISS PEAKE (*leaning forward and speaking in a conspiratorial whisper*) The spare room bed. You know, that big four-poster. Right across the head of the bed under the bolster. Then I remade the bed and lay down on top of it.

(SIR ROWLAND, *flabbergasted, sits above the bridge table*)

CLARISSA. But how did you get the body up to the spare room? You couldn't manage it all by yourself.

MISS PEAKE (*heartily*) You'd be surprised. Good old fireman's lift. Slung it over my shoulder. (*She demonstrates*)

SIR ROWLAND. Supposing you'd met someone, on the stairs?

MISS PEAKE (*rising and crossing to R of Sir Rowland*) Ah, but I didn't. The police were in here with Mrs Hailsham-Brown; you three were in the dining-room. So I grabbed my chance and of course the body, took it through the hall, locked the library door again and popped it up the stairs to the spare room.

SIR ROWLAND. Well, upon my soul!

CLARISSA (*rising*) But he can't stay under the bolster for ever.

MISS PEAKE (*turning to Clarissa*) No, not for ever, of course, Mrs Hailsham-Brown. Twenty-four hours, though. By that time the police will have finished with the house and grounds. (*She moves C*) They'll be looking further afield. Now, I've been thinking. I took out a nice deep trench this morning—for the sweet peas. Well, we'll bury the body there and plant a nice double row of sweet peas all along it.

(CLARISSA, *flabbergasted, sits on the sofa*)

SIR ROWLAND. I'm afraid, Miss Peake, grave digging is no longer a matter for private enterprise.

MISS PEAKE (*laughing heartily*) Oh, you men! (*She wags her finger at Sir Rowland*) Always such sticklers. Now, we've got more sense. (*She leans over the back of the sofa*) We can even take murder in our stride. Eh, Mrs Hailsham-Brown?

HUGO. Of course, she didn't kill him. Don't believe a word of it.

MISS PEAKE (*breezily*) If *she* didn't kill him, who did?

(PIPPA *enters from the hall. She is yawning and walks in a half drunk, sleepy manner. She is carrying a glass dish containing chocolate mousse with a teaspoon in it. They all turn and look at Pippa*)

CLARISSA (*rising; startled*) Pippa! What are you doing out of bed?

PIPPA (*crossing to C; between yawns*) I came down.

(SIR ROWLAND *rises and moves to L of Pippa.* CLARISSA *moves to R of Pippa and leads her to the sofa*)

(*She yawns*) I'm so frightfully hungry. (*To Clarissa. Reproachfully*) You said you'd bring this up.

(CLARISSA *takes the mousse from Pippa, puts it on the stool, then sits Pippa C of the sofa, and sits R of her*)

CLARISSA. I thought you were asleep.

PIPPA (*with an enormous yawn*) I was asleep. Then I thought a policeman came in and looked at me. I'd been having an awful dream and then I half woke up; then I was hungry, so I thought I'd come down. (*She shivers*) Besides, I thought it might be true

SIR ROWLAND (*crossing and sitting* L *of Pippa on the sofa*) What might be true?

PIPPA. That horrible dream about Oliver. (*She shudders*)

SIR ROWLAND. What was your dream about Oliver, Pippa? Tell me.

(PIPPA *takes a small piece of moulded wax from her dressing-gown pocket*)

PIPPA. I made this tonight. I melted down a wax candle, then I made a pin red hot and stuck it through it. (*She gives the figure to Sir Rowland*)

JEREMY. Good Lord! (*He rises and goes around the room, hunting for Pippa's book*)

(MISS PEAKE *moves above the right end of the sofa*)

PIPPA. I said the right words and everything, but I couldn't do it *quite* as the book said.

(JEREMY *looks on the bookshelves up* C *and finds the book*)

CLARISSA. What book? I don't understand.

JEREMY. Here it is. (*He moves to* L *of Miss Peake and hands the book over the back of the sofa to Clarissa*) She got it in the market today. She called it a recipe book.

PIPPA (*with sudden laughter*) And you said, "Can you eat it?"

CLARISSA (*looking at the book*) "A hundred well tried and trusty spells." (*She opens the book*) "How to cure warts; how to get your heart's desire; how to *destroy your enemy.*" Oh, Pippa——

(PIPPA *looks at Clarissa*)

—is that what you did?

PIPPA. Yes.

(CLARISSA *hands the book to Jeremy*)

(*She looks at the wax figure*) It isn't very *like* Oliver and I couldn't get any clippings of his hair. But it was as like him as I could make it—and then—then—I dreamed, I thought—(*she pushes her hair back from her face*) I came down here and he was there. (*She points behind the sofa*) And it was all true.

(SIR ROWLAND *puts the figure on the stool*)

He was there, dead. I *had* killed him. (*She looks around at them*) Is it true? (*She begins to shake*) Did I kill him?

CLARISSA (*putting an arm around Pippa*) No, darling. No.

PIPPA. But he *was* there.

SIR ROWLAND. I know, Pippa, but you didn't kill him. When you stuck the pin through that wax figure, it was your hate and your fear of him you killed that way. You're not afraid of him and you don't hate him any longer. Isn't that true?

PIPPA (*lifting her head and turning to Sir Rowland*) Yes, it's true. But I saw him. (*She glances over the back of the sofa*) I came down here and I saw him lying there, dead. (*She leans her head on Sir Rowland's chest*) I did see him.

SIR ROWLAND. Yes, dear, you did see him. But it wasn't you that killed him. Now, listen to me, Pippa. Somebody hit him over the head with a big stick. You didn't do that, did you?

PIPPA (*looking up*) Oh, no.

(SIR ROWLAND *looks at Clarissa*)

Not a stick. (*She turns to Clarissa*) You mean a golf stick like Jeremy had?

(*There is a slight reaction from Sir Rowland*)

JEREMY. No, not a golf club, Pippa. That big stick that's kept in the hall stand.

PIPPA. The one that belonged to Mr Sellon and Miss Peake calls a knobkerry?

(JEREMY *nods*)

Oh, no, I wouldn't do anything like that. I couldn't. Oh, Uncle Roly, I wouldn't have killed him *really*.

CLARISSA (*with calm common-sense*) Of course you wouldn't.

(JEREMY *sits* R *of the bridge table*)

Now come along, darling, you eat up your chocolate mousse and forget all about it. (*She picks up the dish and offers it to Pippa*)

(PIPPA *refuses the dish which* CLARISSA *replaces on the stool*)

MISS PEAKE. I don't understand a word of all this. (*She crosses to* R *of Jeremy*) What is that book?

(SIR ROWLAND *and* CLARISSA *lie* PIPPA *on the sofa, with her head at the right end.* CLARISSA *stands above the right end of the sofa and takes Pippa's hand.* SIR ROWLAND *stands below the right end of the sofa, and strokes Pippa's hair*)

JEREMY. "How to bring a murrain on your neighbour's cattle." Does that attract you, Miss Peake? I daresay with a little adjusting you could bring black spot to your neighbour's roses.

MISS PEAKE. I don't know what you're talking about.

JEREMY. Black magic.

MISS PEAKE (*moving above the bridge table*) I'm not superstitious, thank goodness.

HUGO. I'm in a complete fog.

MISS PEAKE (*tapping Hugo's shoulder*) Me, too. So I'll just have a peep and see how the boys in blue are getting on.

(MISS PEAKE, *laughing, exits to the hall*)

Sir Rowland. Now where are we?

Clarissa (*crossing to* R *of* Jeremy) What a fool I've been. I should have known Pippa couldn't possibly . . . I didn't know anything about this book. Pippa said she killed him and I—I thought it was true.

Hugo (*rising*) Oh, you mean that you thought Pippa . . . (*He moves down* L)

Clarissa (*moving up* C *and standing with her back to the audience*) Yes, darling.

Hugo. Oh, I see. That explains it. Good God!

Jeremy. Well, we'd better go to the police.

Sir Rowland. I don't know. She's already told them three stories . . .

(Hugo *moves to* L *of the bridge table*)

Clarissa (*turning*) No. Wait. I've got an idea. (*She moves above the bridge table*) Hugo, what was the name of Mr Sellon's shop?

Hugo. It was an antique shop.

Clarissa (*impatiently*) Yes, I know that. But what was it called?

Hugo. What do you mean, "what was it called"?

Clarissa. Oh, dear. You are being difficult. You said it earlier and I want you to say it again. But I don't want to tell you to say it.

(Hugo, Jeremy *and* Sir Rowland *look at each other*)

Hugo. Do you know what the girl is getting at, Roly?

Sir Rowland. No idea. Try again, Clarissa. (*He moves between the stool and the sofa*)

(Pippa *sleeps*)

Clarissa. It's perfectly simple. What was the name of the antique shop?

Hugo. It hadn't got a name. I mean, antique shops aren't called "Seaview" or anything.

Clarissa. Heaven give me patience. What was written up over the door?

Hugo. Written up? Nothing. What should be written up? Only "Sellon and Brown", of course.

Clarissa. At last. I thought that was what you said before, but I wasn't sure. Sellon and Brown. *My* name is Hailsham-*Brown*— (*she crosses to* L *of Sir Rowland*) we got this house dirt cheap; other people who came to see it before us were asked such an exhorbitant rent that they went away in disgust. Now have you got there?

Hugo (*moving down* L *of the bridge table*) No.

Jeremy (*rising and tucking his chair under the table*) Not yet.

Sir Rowland. In a glass, dimly.

CLARISSA. Mr Sellon's partner who lives in London is a woman. Today someone rang up and asked to speak to Mrs Brown. Not Mrs Hailsham-Brown, just Mrs Brown.

SIR ROWLAND. I see what you're getting at.

HUGO. I don't.

CLARISSA (*looking at Hugo*) A horse chestnut or a chestnut horse—one of them makes all the difference.

HUGO (*with a step towards Clarissa*) You're not delirious or anything, are you, Clarissa?

CLARISSA. Somebody killed Oliver. It wasn't any of you three; it wasn't me or Henry—(*she turns to Sir Rowland*) it wasn't Pippa —thank God—then who was it?

SIR ROWLAND. It's as I said to the Inspector. An outside job. Someone followed Oliver here.

CLARISSA. But *why* did they? When I left you at the gate today, I came back and in through that window and Oliver was standing near that desk. He was very surprised to see me. He said, "What are you doing here, Clarissa?" I just thought it was an elaborate way of annoying me. But suppose it was just what it seemed? He *was* surprised to see me. He thought the house belonged to someone else. He thought the person he'd find here would be the Mrs Brown who was Mr Sellon's partner.

SIR ROWLAND. Wouldn't he know that you and Henry had this house? Wouldn't Miranda know?

CLARISSA. When Miranda has to communicate she always does it through her lawyers. I tell you, Oliver had no idea he was going to see me. Oh, he recovered pretty quickly and made the excuse that he'd come to talk about Pippa. Then he pretended to go away but he came back because . . .

(MISS PEAKE *enters from the hall and stands above the bridge table.* HUGO *sits in the easy chair.* SIR ROWLAND *moves above the table* R *of the sofa.* JEREMY *stands above the left end of the sofa*)

MISS PEAKE. The hunt's still on. They've looked under all the beds, I gather, and now they're out in the grounds. (*She laughs*)

CLARISSA (*moving up* C *level with Miss Peake*) Miss Peake, do you remember what Mr Costello said just before he left. Do you?

MISS PEAKE. Haven't an idea.

CLARISSA. He said, didn't he, "I came to see Mrs Brown"?

MISS PEAKE. I believe he did. Yes. Why?

CLARISSA. But it wasn't me he came to see.

MISS PEAKE. Well, if it wasn't you, then I don't know who it was. (*She laughs*)

CLARISSA (*with emphasis*) It was *you*. You're Mrs Brown, aren't you?

(MISS PEAKE *is startled, unaware for a moment how to act. When she does speak, her manner has changed. She speaks gravely, and has dropped the jolly, hearty touch)*

MISS PEAKE. That's bright of you. Yes. I'm Mrs Brown.

CLARISSA. You're Mr Sellon's partner. You own this house; you inherited it with the business. You had the idea of finding a tenant for it whose name was Brown. You thought that wouldn't be too difficult. In the end you compromised on Hailsham-Brown. I don't know exactly why you wanted me to be in the limelight whilst you watched. I don't understand the ins and outs . . .

MISS PEAKE. Charles Sellon was murdered. He'd got hold of something that was very valuable. I don't know how—I don't even know what it was. He wasn't always very—(*she hesitates*) scrupulous.

SIR ROWLAND (*with a step behind the sofa*) So we have heard.

MISS PEAKE. Whatever it was, he was killed for it. And whoever killed him didn't find the thing. Probably because it wasn't in the shop, it was *here*. I thought whoever it was who killed him would come here sooner or later. I wanted to be on the watch, therefore I wanted a dummy Mrs Brown.

(JEREMY *backs below the panel*)

SIR ROWLAND (*with feeling*) It didn't worry you that Mrs Hailsham-Brown, a perfectly innocent woman, would be in danger?

MISS PEAKE. I've kept an eye on her, haven't I? So much so that it annoyed you all sometimes. The other day when a man came along and offered her a ridiculous price for that desk I was sure I was on the right track. Yet I'll swear there was nothing in that desk that meant anything at all.

SIR ROWLAND. Did you examine the secret drawer?

MISS PEAKE (*with a step towards Clarissa*) A secret drawer, is there?

CLARISSA (*intercepting Miss Peake*) There's nothing there now. Pippa found the drawer but there were only some old autographs in it.

SIR ROWLAND. Clarissa, I'd rather like to see those autographs again.

(CLARISSA *moves to* L *of Sir Rowland and leans over the back of the sofa*)

CLARISSA. Pippa, where did you put . . .? Oh, she's asleep.

MISS PEAKE (*moving to* L *of the sofa*) Fast asleep. That's all the excitement. Tell you what, I'll carry her up and dump her on her bed.

SIR ROWLAND (*leaning over the back of the sofa and touching Pippa*) No.

Miss Peake. She's no weight. Not a quarter as heavy as the late Mr Costello.

Sir Rowland. All the same, I think she'll be safer here.

Clarissa. Safer? (*She turns sharply to Miss Peake*)

(*The others all look at Miss Peake*)

Miss Peake (*backing a step and looking around*) Safer?

Sir Rowland. That's what I said. That child said a very significant thing just now. (*He crosses above Clarissa and sits above the bridge table*)

(*They all watch Sir Rowland. There is a pause*)

Hugo (*rising and moving to L of the bridge table*) What did she say? (*He sits L of the table*)

Sir Rowland. If you all think back, perhaps you'll realize it.

(*The others look at each other. Sir Rowland picks up the copy of "Who's Who" and looks at it*)

Hugo (*shaking his head*) I don't get it.

Jeremy. What did she say?

Clarissa (*frowning*) I can't imagine. The policeman? Dreaming? Coming down here? Half awake?

Hugo. Don't be damned mysterious, Roly. What is all this?

Sir Rowland (*looking up from the book; absent-mindedly*) What? Oh, yes. Those autographs. Where are they?

Hugo. I believe I remember Pippa putting them in that shell box over there.

Jeremy (*moving to the bookshelves up c*) Up here?

(Miss Peake *moves above the left end of the sofa.* Jeremy *opens the shell box and takes out the envelope. He waits just a second, catching his breath, as he looks inside.* Sir Rowland *closes "Who's Who"*)

Quite right. There we are. (*He takes the autographs from the envelope, hands them to Sir Rowland, at the same time slipping the envelope into his pocket. He then backs up* c)

Sir Rowland (*examining the autographs with his eye-glass*) Victoria R, God bless her.

(Miss Peake *crosses to* R *of the bridge table.* Clarissa *follows and stands between Sir Rowland and Miss Peake.* Jeremy *moves behind Clarissa*)

Faded brown ink. John Ruskin—yes, authentic, I should say. Robert Browning—paper not as old as it ought to be.

Clarissa (*excitedly*) Roly! What do you mean?

Sir Rowland. I had some experience of invisible inks and that sort of thing, during the war. If you wanted to make a secret note of something, it wouldn't be a bad idea to write it in invisible ink on a sheet of paper and then fake an autograph. Put that autograph with other genuine autographs and nobody would notice it or look at it twice, probably. Any more than we did.

Miss Peake. But what *could* Charles Sellon have written which would be worth fourteen thousand pounds?

Sir Rowland. Nothing at all, dear lady. But it occurs to me, you know, that it might have been a question of safety.

Miss Peake. Safety?

Sir Rowland. Costello is suspected of supplying drugs. Sellon, so the Inspector tells us, was questioned once or twice by the Narcotic Squad. There's a connexion there, don't you think? But, of course, it might be just a foolish idea of mine. (*He looks down at the paper*) I don't think it would be anything elaborate on Sellon's part. Lemon juice perhaps, or a solution of barium chloride. Gentle heat might do the trick. We can always try iodine vapour later. Yes, a little gentle heat. (*He rises*) Shall we try the experiment?

Clarissa. There's an electric fire in the library.

(Hugo *rises and tucks in his chair*)

Jeremy, will you get it?

(Jeremy *exits to the library*)

We can plug it in here.

Miss Peake (*moving below the panel*) The whole thing's ridiculous. Too far fetched for words.

Clarissa. I think it's a wonderful idea.

(Jeremy *enters from the library, carrying a small electric radiator*)

Got it?

Jeremy. Here it is. Where's the plug?

Clarissa (*taking the radiator from Jeremy and pointing up* c) Down there.

(Jeremy *plugs the lead into the skirting* r *of the library door.* Clarissa *puts the radiator on the floor up* c. Sir Rowland *takes the Robert Browning autograph and stands* l *of the radiator, with* Clarissa *below him.* Jeremy *kneels above the radiator and* Miss Peake *stands* r *of it*)

Sir Rowland. We mustn't hope for too much. After all, it's only an idea——

(Hugo *tucks in the chair above the bridge table*)

—but there must have been some very good reason why Sellon kept these bits of paper in such a secret place.

Hugo (*moving to* l *of Clarissa*) Takes me back years. I remember writing secret messages with lemon juice when I was a kid.

Jeremy. Which shall we start with?

Clarissa. Queen Victoria.

JEREMY. Six to one, Ruskin.

SIR ROWLAND. I'm putting my money on Robert Browning. (*He bends over and holds the paper in front of the radiator*)

HUGO. Most obscure chap—never could understand a word of his poetry.

SIR ROWLAND. Exactly. Full of hidden meaning.

(*They all crane over Sir Rowland*)

CLARISSA. I can't bear it if nothing happens.

SIR ROWLAND. I believe—yes.

JEREMY Yes, there is something coming up.

CLARISSA. Is there! Let me see.

HUGO (*pushing between Clarissa and Jeremy*) Move above, young man.

SIR ROWLAND. Steady. Don't joggle me—yes—there *is* writing. (*He straightens up*) We've got it.

MISS PEAKE. What have you got?

(SIR ROWLAND *moves down* C. *The others follow.* JEREMY *goes to* R *of Sir Rowland,* MISS PEAKE *to* R *of Jeremy,* CLARISSA *and* HUGO *to* L *of Sir Rowland*)

SIR ROWLAND. A list of six names and addresses. Distributors in the drug racket I should say; and one of those names is *Oliver Costello.*

(*All exclaim*)

CLARISSA. Oliver! So that's why he came and someone must have followed him and . . . Oh, Uncle Roly, we must tell the police. Come along, Hugo.

(CLARISSA *rushes to the hall door, followed by* HUGO. SIR ROWLAND *picks up the other autographs.*

JEREMY *unplugs the radiator and exits with it to the library.* MISS PEAKE *starts towards the hall door, then turns back to* PIPPA)

HUGO (*as he goes*) Most extraordinary thing I ever heard of.

(CLARISSA *and* HUGO *exit to the hall*)

SIR ROWLAND (*pausing in the hall doorway*) Coming, Miss Peake?

MISS PEAKE. You don't want me, do you?

SIR ROWLAND. I think we do. You were Sellon's partner.

MISS PEAKE. I've never had anything to do with the drug business. I ran the antique side—(*she crosses to the hall door*) did all the London buying and selling.

SIR ROWLAND. I see.

(SIR ROWLAND *exits to the hall.* MISS PEAKE *looks back at* PIPPA *for a moment, then turns out the wall-brackets and exits to the hall.*

JEREMY *enters from the library. He moves down* C, *glances at*

Pippa, then crosses to the easy chair down L, picks up the cushion from it and moves slowly behind the sofa. Pippa stirs in her sleep. Jeremy stands frozen for a moment, then he continues till he stands behind Pippa's head and slowly lowers the cushion over her face.
Clarissa *enters from the hall)*

Clarissa. Hullo, Jeremy. (*She closes the hall door)*

(Jeremy, *on hearing the door, carefully places the cushion over Pippa's feet)*

Jeremy. I remembered what Sir Rowland said, so I thought perhaps we oughtn't to leave Pippa all alone. Her feet seemed a bit cold, so I was just covering them up.

Clarissa (*crossing to the stool)* All this excitement has made me feel terribly hungry. (*She looks at the plate of sandwiches. Disappointed)* Oh, Jeremy. You've eaten them all.

Jeremy. Sorry, but I was starving.

Clarissa (*moving above the left end of the sofa)* I don't see why you should be. You've had dinner. I haven't.

Jeremy (*sitting on the back of the sofa at the right end)* I haven't had dinner either. I was practising approach shots. I only came into the dining-room just after your telephone call came.

Clarissa (*negligently)* Oh, I see. (*She bends over the back of the sofa to pat the cushion. Suddenly her eyes widen. In a deeply moved voice)* I see—you . . .

Jeremy. What do you mean?

Clarissa (*almost to herself)* You!

Jeremy. What did you mean by "You!"?

Clarissa. What were you doing with that cushion when I came into the room?

Jeremy. I was covering up Pippa's feet. They were cold.

Clarissa. Were you? Is that really what you were going to do? Or were you going to put that cushion over her mouth?

Jeremy. Clarissa!

Clarissa. I said none of us could have killed him. But one of us could. You. You were out on the golf course alone. You could have come back to the house, in through the library window, which you'd left open, you had your golf club still in your hand. That's what Pippa saw. That's what she meant when she said, "A golf stick like Jeremy had." She *saw* you.

Jeremy. That's nonsense, Clarissa.

Clarissa. No, it isn't. Then after you'd killed Oliver you went back to the club and rang the police so that they should come here, find the body and think it was Henry or I had killed him.

Jeremy (*rising and moving down R of the sofa)* What absolute rubbish!

Clarissa. It's true. I know it's true. (*She moves down L of the sofa)* But why? That's what I don't understand. Why?

(JEREMY *takes the envelope from his pocket, crosses between the sofa and stool to Clarissa, and holds out the envelope, but does not let Clarissa take it*)

JEREMY. This.

CLARISSA. That's the envelope the autographs were kept in.

JEREMY. There's a stamp on it. It's what's known as an error stamp. Printed in the wrong colour. One from Sweden sold last year for fourteen thousand three hundred pounds.

CLARISSA (*stepping back*) So that's it.

JEREMY. This stamp came into Sellon's possession. He wrote to my boss about it. I opened the letter. I came down and saw Sellon . . .

CLARISSA. And killed him.

(JEREMY *nods*)

But you couldn't find the stamp.

JEREMY. No. It wasn't in the shop so I felt sure it must be here——(*he circles round to up L of Clarissa*)

(CLARISSA *backs towards the left arm of the sofa*)

—and tonight I thought Costello had beaten me to it.

CLARISSA. And so you killed him, too.

(JEREMY *nods*)

And just now you would have killed Pippa?

JEREMY. Why not?

CLARISSA. I can't believe it.

JEREMY. My dear Clarissa, fourteen thousand pounds is a great deal of money.

CLARISSA. But why are you telling me this? Do you imagine for one moment that I shan't go to the police?

JEREMY. They'll never believe you.

CLARISSA. Oh yes, they will.

JEREMY. Besides, you're not going to get the chance. (*He advances on her*) Do you think that when I've killed two people I shall worry about killing a third? (*He grips Clarissa by the throat*)

(CLARISSA *screams*.
      SIR ROWLAND *enters from the hall and switches on the wall-brackets*.
      The CONSTABLE *enters by the french windows*.
      The INSPECTOR *enters from the library*)

INSPECTOR (*grabbing Jeremy*) All right, Warrender. Thank you. That's just the evidence we need. Give me that envelope.

(CLARISSA *backs behind the sofa, holding her throat*)

JEREMY (*handing the envelope to the Inspector*) A trap. Very clever.

INSPECTOR. Jeremy Warrender, I arrest you for the murder of Oliver Costello, and I must warn you that anything you say may be taken down and may be given in evidence.

(*The* CONSTABLE *moves to* R *of Jeremy*)

JEREMY. You can save your breath, Inspector. It was a good gamble.

INSPECTOR (*backing up* C *a step*) Take him away.

(*The* CONSTABLE *takes Jeremy's arm*)

JEREMY. Forgotten your handcuffs, Mr Jones?

(*The* CONSTABLE *twists* JEREMY'S *right arm behind his back and marches him off by the french windows*)

SIR ROWLAND (*crossing to Clarissa*) Are you all right, my dear?
CLARISSA. Yes, yes, I'm all right.
SIR ROWLAND. I never meant to expose you to this.
CLARISSA. You knew it was Jeremy, didn't you?
INSPECTOR (*moving to* L *of Sir Rowland*) But what made you think of the stamp, sir?
SIR ROWLAND (*moving to the Inspector and taking the envelope from him*) Well, Inspector, it rang a bell when Pippa gave me the envelope this evening. Then when I found from *Who's Who* that Sir Lazarus Stein was a stamp collector my suspicion developed, and just now when he had the impertinence to pocket the envelope under my nose, I felt it was a certainty. (*He returns the envelope to the Inspector*) Take great care of it, Inspector, you'll probably find it's extremely valuable, besides being evidence.
INSPECTOR. It's evidence all right. A particularly vicious young criminal is going to get his deserts.

(SIR ROWLAND *moves up* C)

(*He crosses to the hall door*) However, we've still got to find the body.
CLARISSA (*crossing to* C) Oh, that's easy, Inspector. Look in the spare room bed.
INSPECTOR (*moving to* L *of Clarissa; disapprovingly*) Now really, Mrs Hailsham-Brown . . .
CLARISSA. Why does nobody ever believe me? It is in the spare room bed. You go and look, Inspector. Across the bed, under the bolster. Miss Peake put it there, trying to be kind.
INSPECTOR. Trying to be . . .? (*He breaks off, moves to the hall door and turns. Reproachfully*) You know, Mrs Hailsham-Brown, you haven't made things easier for us tonight; telling us all these tall stories. I suppose you thought your husband had done it, and were lying to cover up for him. But you shouldn't do it, madam. You really shouldn't do it.

(*The* INSPECTOR *exits to the hall*)

CLARISSA. Well! (*She moves below the sofa*) Oh, Pippa . . .
SIR ROWLAND (*moving above the sofa and bending over the back*)
Better get her up to bed. She'll be safe now.
CLARISSA (*gently shaking Pippa*) Come on, Pippa. Ups-a-daisy.
Time you were in bed.

(PIPPA *gets up, waveringly*)

PIPPA (*murmuring*) Hungry.
CLARISSA (*leading Pippa to the hall door*) Yes, yes, I know. We'll
see what we can find.
SIR ROWLAND. Good night, Pippa.
PIPPA. Good night.

(CLARISSA and PIPPA *exit to the hall.* SIR ROWLAND *sits* R *of the
bridge table and puts the cards in their boxes*)

HUGO (*off*) Can I help you, Clarissa?
CLARISSA (*off*) No, thank you. I can manage.

(HUGO *enters from the hall*)

HUGO (*moving up* R *of Sir Rowland*) God bless my soul! I'd
never have believed it. Seemed a decent enough young fellow.
Been to a good school. Knew all the right people.
SIR ROWLAND. But was quite willing to commit murder for the
sake of fourteen thousand pounds. It happens now and then,
Hugo, in every class of society. An attractive personality and no
moral sense.

(MISS PEAKE *enters from the hall*)

MISS PEAKE (*moving up* L *of the bridge table*) I thought I'd just
tell you, Sir Rowland, I've got to go along to the police station.
They want me to make a statement. They're not too pleased at
the trick I played them, I'm in for a wigging, I'm afraid.

(MISS PEAKE *roars with laughter and exits to the hall*)

HUGO (*moving down* R *of Sir Rowland*) You know, Roly, I don't
quite get it. Was Miss Peake Mrs Sellon, or was Mr Sellon—
Mr Brown? Or the other way round?

(*The* INSPECTOR *enters from the hall*)

INSPECTOR. We're removing the body now, sir. (*He picks up his
cap and gloves*)

(HUGO *moves up* C)

SIR ROWLAND. Oh yes, Inspector.
INSPECTOR (*moving to* L *of the bridge table*) Would you mind
advising Mrs Hailsham-Brown that if she tells these fancy stories
to the police, one day she'll get into real trouble.
SIR ROWLAND (*gently*) She did actually tell you the true story

once, you know, Inspector. But you simply wouldn't believe her.

INSPECTOR. Yes—hmmm—well. Frankly, sir, it was a bit difficult to swallow, you'll admit.

SIR ROWLAND. Oh, I admit it.

INSPECTOR (*confidentially*) Not that I blame you, sir. Mrs Hailsham-Brown is a lady with a very taking way with her. Good night, sir.

SIR ROWLAND. Good night, Inspector.

INSPECTOR (*backing to the hall door*) Good night, Mr Birch.

HUGO (*beckoning the Inspector to him*) Well done, Inspector. (*He holds out his hand*)

INSPECTOR (*shaking hands with Hugo*) Oh, thank you, sir.

(*The* INSPECTOR *smiles, then looks at* SIR ROWLAND *and his smile fades.* SIR ROWLAND *looks down, trying not to smile.*
The INSPECTOR *exits to the hall.* HUGO *yawns*)

HUGO. Oh, well. Suppose I'd better be going home to bed. Some evening, eh?

SIR ROWLAND (*tidying the bridge table*) As you say, Hugo, some evening. Good night.

HUGO. Good night.

(HUGO *exits to the hall.* SIR ROWLAND *leaves the cards and markers in a neat pile on the table, then rises, picks up "Who's Who", moves up* C *and puts it on the bookshelves.*
CLARISSA *enters from the hall*)

CLARISSA (*moving to Sir Rowland and putting her hands on his arms*) Darling Roly. And so clever, too.

SIR ROWLAND. You lucky young woman. A good thing you didn't lose your heart to that young man.

CLARISSA. If I lost my heart to anybody, darling, it would be to you.

SIR ROWLAND. Now, now, none of your tricks with me.

(HENRY *enters by the french windows*)

CLARISSA (*startled*) Henry!

HENRY (*moving below the right end of the sofa; preoccupied*) Hullo, Roly. Thought you were at the club tonight?

SIR ROWLAND. Well—er—I thought I'd turn in early. It's been rather a strenuous evening. (*He crosses to the hall doors*)

HENRY (*looking at the bridge table*) Bridge?

SIR ROWLAND. Bridge and—(*he smiles*) er—other things. Good night.

(CLARISSA *blows a kiss to Sir Rowland.*
SIR ROWLAND *blows a kiss to Clarissa and exits to the hall*)

CLARISSA (*moving to* L *of Henry; eagerly*) Where's Kalen—Mr Jones?

HENRY (*putting his brief-case on the sofa; with weary disgust*) He didn't come.

CLARISSA. What!

HENRY (*unbuttoning his overcoat*) The plane arrived with nothing but a half-baked aide-de-camp in it.

(CLARISSA *helps Henry off with his overcoat*)

First thing he did was to turn round and fly back again where he'd come from.

CLARISSA. Why?

HENRY. How do I know? Suspicious, it seems. Suspicious of what? I ask you?

CLARISSA (*removing Henry's hat*) But what about Sir John?

HENRY. That's the worst of it. He'll be arriving down any minute now, I expect. (*He consults his watch*) Of course I rang up at once from the aerodrome, but he'd already started. Oh, the whole thing's a most ghastly fiasco. (*He sinks on to the sofa*)

(*The telephone rings*)

CLARISSA (*crossing to the telephone*) I'll answer it. It may be the police. (*She lifts the receiver*)

HENRY. The police?

CLARISSA (*into the telephone*) Yes . . . Yes, this is Copplestone Court . . . Yes, he's here. (*To Henry*) It's for you, darling. Bindley Heath aerodrome.

(HENRY *rises, rushes across to the telephone, but half-way over, stops and proceeds at a dignified walk*)

HENRY (*into the telephone*) Hullo? . . .

(CLARISSA *exits to the hall with the hat and coat, but re-enters immediately and stands behind Henry*)

Yes—speaking . . . *What?* . . . Ten minutes later? . . . Shall I? . . . Yes . . . Yes, yes . . . No . . . No, no . . . You have? . . . I see . . . Yes . . . Right. (*He replaces the receiver and shouts*) Clarissa! (*He turns and sees her behind him*) Oh. Another plane came in just ten minutes after the first and Kalendorff was on it.

CLARISSA. Mr Jones, you mean.

HENRY. Quite right, darling. One can't be too careful. Yes, it seems that the first plane was a kind of security precaution. Really, one can't fathom how these people's minds work. Well, anyway, they're sending him over here now with an R.A.F. escort. He'll be here in about a quarter of an hour. Now then, is everything all right? Get rid of those cards, will you?

(CLARISSA *hurriedly collects the cards and markers and puts them on the table up* C. HENRY *crosses to the stool, picks up the sandwich plate and mousse dish with an air of great surprise*)

What's this?

CLARISSA (*rushing to Henry and seizing the plate and dish*) Pippa was eating it. I'll take it away. I'll go and make some more ham sandwiches.

HENRY. Not yet—the chairs. (*Slightly reproachful*) I thought you were going to have everything ready? (*He crosses to the bridge table and folds the legs*)

(CLARISSA *puts the plate and dish on the stool, then moves the chair above the bridge table to* R *of the table up* C)

What have you been doing all the evening? (*He puts the bridge table in the library*)

CLARISSA (*crossing to the easy chair and pushing it forward*) Oh, Henry, it's been the most terribly exciting evening. You see, I came in here with some sandwiches soon after you left, and the first thing that happened was I fell over a body. There—behind the sofa.

HENRY (*crossing to the easy chair, interrupting*) Yes, yes, darling.

(HENRY *and* CLARISSA *push the easy chair into its original position*)

Your stories are always enchanting, but really there isn't time now.

(CLARISSA *takes the chair from* R *of the bridge table and puts it down* R. HENRY *takes the chair* L *of the bridge table and puts it down* L. *They both go to the armchair and push it down to its original position*)

CLARISSA. But, Henry, it's *true*. That's only the beginning. The police came and it was just one thing after another. There was a narcotic ring; and Miss Peake isn't Miss Peake, she's really Mrs Brown, and Jeremy turned out to be the murderer and he was trying to steal a stamp worth fourteen thousand pounds.

HENRY (*moving to* L *of the armchair; indulgent, but not really listening*) Hmm! Must have been a second Swedish yellow.

CLARISSA (*moving to* R *of the armchair*) That's just what it was.

HENRY (*affectionately*) The things you imagine, Clarissa. (*He moves the small table from* L, *sets it between the armchair and easy chair and flicks the crumbs off it with his handkerchief*)

CLARISSA. But, darling, I didn't imagine it. I couldn't have imagined half as much.

(HENRY *crosses behind the sofa, puts his brief-case behind the right cushion, plumps up the left cushion, then picks up the easy chair cushion and crosses with it to the easy chair*)

How extraordinary it is; all my life nothing has really happened to me and tonight I've had the lot. Murder, police, drug addicts, invisible ink, secret writing, almost arrested for manslaughter and very nearly murdered. You know, in a way, it's almost *too* much all in one evening.

HENRY (*moving to* L *of the armchair*) Do go and make that coffee, darling. You can tell me all your lovely rigmarole tomorrow.

CLARISSA. But don't you realize, Henry, that *I* was nearly murdered?

HENRY (*looking at his watch*) Either Sir John or Mr Jones might arrive at any minute.

CLARISSA. What I've been through this evening. Oh, dear, it reminds me of Sir Walter Scott.

HENRY (*moving down* L *and looking around the room*) What does?

CLARISSA. My aunt made me learn it by heart.

(HENRY *looks at Clarissa*)

(*She quotes*) "Oh, what a tangled web we weave, when first we practise to deceive."

(HENRY, *suddenly conscious of Clarissa, leans over the armchair and puts his arms around her*)

HENRY. My adorable spider!

CLARISSA (*her arms on his shoulders*) Do you know the facts of life about spiders? They eat their husbands. (*She scrabbles his neck with her fingers*)

HENRY (*with passion*) I'm more likely to eat you. (*He kisses her*)

(*The front door bell rings off*)

CLARISSA (*starting away*) Sir Jones!

HENRY (*at the same time*) Mr John!

CLARISSA (*pushing Henry to the hall door*) You go out and answer the front door.

(HENRY *buttons up his jacket and straightens his tie*)

I'll put coffee and sandwiches in the hall and you can bring them in when you want them. High level talks will now begin. (*She kisses her hand, then puts her hand to his mouth*) Good luck, darling.

HENRY. Good luck. (*He turns away, then turns back again*) I mean, thanks.

(HENRY *exits to the hall, leaving the door open.* CLARISSA *picks up the plate and dish*)

(*Off*) Good evening, Sir John.

(CLARISSA *moves towards the hall doors, stops, hesitates, then goes to the bookshelves up* C *and actuates the panel switch. The panel opens. The front door slams off*)

CLARISSA (*dramatically*) Exit Clarissa mysteriously.

CLARISSA *disappears into the recess as—*

the CURTAIN *falls*

FURNITURE AND PROPERTY PLOT

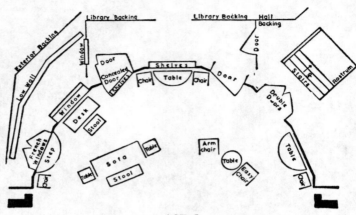

ACT I

On stage—Sofa. *On it:* 2 cushions

Small table (L of sofa). *On it:* silver cigarette box with cigarettes, matches, ashtray, table-lighter

Small table (R of sofa). *On it:* ashtray

Long stool. *On it:* copy of *The Times*

Armchair (LC)

Easy chair. *On it:* cushion

Small table (LC)

Console table (L). *On it:* tray with 3 glasses of port, marked one, two and three; piece of writing-paper, pencil, telephone, telephone directory, pot of tulips

Desk with secret drawer. *On it:* table-lamp, books, copy of *Who's Who*, blotter, fountain pen, ashtray

In centre pigeon-hole: notepaper and envelopes

In centre drawer: copy of agreement

In secret drawer: piece of paper "Sucks to you"

Desk stool

Waste-paper basket

Console table (up C). *On it:* open box of chocolates

4 upright chairs

On panel shelves: ornaments, books

On built-in bookshelves: switch or lever for panel, books, spray of daffodils, ornaments, shell box with envelope containing 3 pieces of autographed paper; 4 bridge markers with pencils, 2 packs of cards, one red backed and one blue

2 pairs window curtains and pelmets

Carpet on floor

Rug at library door

Runner in hall

Runner in library

Stair carpet

Picture on wall L.
4 pairs electric-candle wall-brackets
Switches above and below hall door
Concealed lighting in cornice
3-pin socket in skirting R of library door

Window curtains open
French windows open
Doors closed
Panel closed
Light fittings off
Console table L set at right angles to wall
Set knobkerry in secret recess after murder

Off stage—Gumboots, broccoli (MISS PEAKE)
    Gardening fork (MISS PEAKE)
    Torch (OLIVER)
    Hat, satchel with old book and school books (PIPPA)
    Bun (PIPPA)
    Tray. *On it:* 4 glasses, syphon of soda, bottle of whisky, bottle of
        brandy (ELGIN)
    Plate of sandwiches in napkin (CLARISSA)
    Golf club, 2 golf balls, golfing gloves (JEREMY)
    Brief-case (HENRY)
    Black coat, mask and glove for murderer

Personal—SIR ROWLAND: blindfold, eye-glass, pencil, handkerchief
    OLIVER: case with cigarettes
    HENRY: horn-rimmed spectacles, empty cigarette case
    CLARISSA: wedding ring, watch, handkerchief

The sound of the murder may be made, off stage R, by hitting a coconut, in a heavy linen bag, with a wooden mallet.

ACT II

SCENE 1

Strike—Chocolates, pencil and paper, dirty glasses

Set—Folding card table LC. *On it:* 2 packs playing cards, 4 hands laid out,
    4 markers and pencils

4 upright chairs around card table
2 clean glasses on tray up c
Torch and "Sucks to you" behind sofa
   3 pairs washleather gloves under left cushion of sofa

Move easy chair down L
Move armchair above hall doors
Move table LC to L
Move telephone to upstage end of table
Move desk stool under desk

Check red Ace of Spades under left end of sofa
Check knobkerry in secret recess

Window curtains closed
French windows open
Doors closed
Panel closed
Light fittings on
Desk lamp on

Off stage—Gloves, car registration book (CONSTABLE)

Personal—MISS PEAKE: towel
      JEREMY: golfing gloves
      CONSTABLE: notebook, pencil, penknife

SCENE 2

Move chair from below card table to L of table up c
Hand glass of brandy to Sir Rowland

Window curtains closed
French windows open
Doors closed
Panel open
Light fittings on
Desk lamp on

At cue—Take knobkerry and torch from secret recess
      Check "Sucks to you" in secret recess

ACT III

Strike—Brandy glass, 3 pairs of gloves, Constable's hat

Move desk stool under desk
Push chairs under card table
Tidy card table
Window curtains closed
French windows open
Library door closed
Hall doors open
Panel closed
Light fittings on
Desk lamp on

Off stage—Chocolate mousse and spoon in glass dish (PIPPA)
      Wax figure (PIPPA)
      Brief-case (HENRY)
      In library: portable electric radiator with flex and 3-pin plug
        (JEREMY)

LIGHTING PLOT

Property Fittings Required—4 pairs electric-candle wall-brackets, table-lamp, portable electric radiator, concealed light fittings (all practical)

Interior. A drawing-room. The same scene throughout
THE MAIN ACTING AREAS ARE—at a sofa (RC), a desk (up R), chairs LC and L and areas up RC, up C and down C

ACT I   A March evening

THE APPARENT SOURCES OF LIGHT ARE—in daylight—french windows and a sash window R; at night—wall-brackets down R, up R, up L and down L, concealed lighting in the cornice and a table-lamp up R

To open: Daylight effect outside windows
Floods on library backings up RC and up LC
Flood in hall L
Fittings off

Cue 1	MISS PEAKE: Ahoy there!	*Commence slow fade exterior lighting—15 mins.—to moonlight*	(page 7)

Cue 1   MISS PEAKE: Ahoy there!   (page 7)
Commence slow fade exterior lighting—15 mins.—to moonlight

Cue 2   CLARISSA: And shut the door   (page 11)
Commence slow fade interior lighting—11 mins.—overlaps Cue 1

Cue 3   CLARISSA switches on the concealed lighting   (page 21)
Snap on strip lighting
Bring up interior lights a little

Cue 4   HENRY switches on the wall-brackets   (page 21)
Snap on wall-brackets
Bring up interior lights

Cue 5   HENRY switches off the concealed lighting   (page 23)
Snap out strip lighting
Reduce interior lights a little

Cue 6   HENRY switches off wall-brackets   (page 24)
Snap out wall-brackets
BLACK-OUT all lights except moonlight through windows R

Cue 7   HENRY switches on wall-brackets   (page 24)
Snap on wall-brackets
Bring up on-stage lights

ACT II   SCENE 1   Evening

To open: Moonlight outside windows
Wall-brackets on
Table-lamp on
Concealed lighting on
Floods in library on
Hall flood on

Cue 8   INSPECTOR: So there was a murder here tonight   (page 45)
Quick dim to BLACK-OUT

ACT II   SCENE 2   Evening

To open: Moonlight outside windows
Wall-brackets on
Table-lamp on

Concealed lighting on
Floods in library on
Hall flood on

No cues

ACT III   Evening

To open: Moonlight outside windows
Wall-brackets on
Table-lamp on
Concealed lighting on
Floods in library on
Hall flood on

Cue 9   MISS PEAKE switches out wall-brackets   (page 78)
Snap out wall-brackets
Reduce interior lights

Cue 10   SIR ROWLAND *switches on wall-brackets*   (page 80)
Snap on wall-brackets
Bring up interior lights

MADE AND PRINTED IN GREAT BRITAIN BY
LATIMER TREND & COMPANY LTD PLYMOUTH
MADE IN ENGLAND